United States, S. Beckley Holabird

Flags of the Army of the United States

carried during the War of the Rebellion, 1861-1865

United States, S. Beckley Holabird

Flags of the Army of the United States
carried during the War of the Rebellion, 1861-1865

ISBN/EAN: 9783337119553

Printed in Europe, USA, Canada, Australia, Japan

Cover: Foto ©ninafisch / pixelio.de

More available books at **www.hansebooks.com**

FLAGS
OF THE
ARMY OF THE UNITED STATES
CARRIED DURING
The War OF THE Rebellion
1861-1865,

to designate the Headquarters
of the different
Armies, Army Corps, Divisions and Brigades.

Compiled under direction of the
Quartermaster General U.S. Army.

1887

Copyright, 1886, by
Brig. Gen. S. B. HOLABIRD
Q. M. Gen., U. S. A.

✣ NOTE ✣

The illustrations contained in this volume are based upon official orders, and such other data as the Quartermaster's Department has been able to gather through private correspondence. It has not been practicable to obtain definite information in all cases, and the Quartermaster-General will be thankful for any authentic correction of errors.

A LIMITED edition of this work, "**Flags of the Army of the United States** carried during the war of the Rebellion, 1861–1865, to designate the Headquarters of the different Armies, Army Corps, Divisions and Brigades, compiled under direction of the Quartermaster-General, U. S. A., 1887," is for sale by the undersigned, delivered free by mail to any part of the United States on receipt of price........................... $5 00

ALSO

"**Commanders of Army Corps, Divisions and Brigades**, United States Army during the War of 1861 to 1865, size of double page 17¼ × 22¾ inches, heavy ledger paper, bound in cloth in folio (atlas) style 12½ × 17½ inches, price............. 5 00

OR

The above two works, strongly bound together in one folio volume (13 × 18 ins.) in Cloth... 9 00
In Half Turkey Morocco... 10 00

BURK & McFETRIDGE,
PRINTERS, LITHOGRAPHERS AND PUBLISHERS,
NOS. 306 AND 308 CHESTNUT STREET, PHILADELPHIA.

GEN. GRANT'S HEADQUARTERS

GEN. SHERMAN'S HEADQUARTERS.

FLAG USED AT GEN. SHERMAN'S HEADQUARTERS.

GEN. SHERIDAN'S BATTLE FLAG.

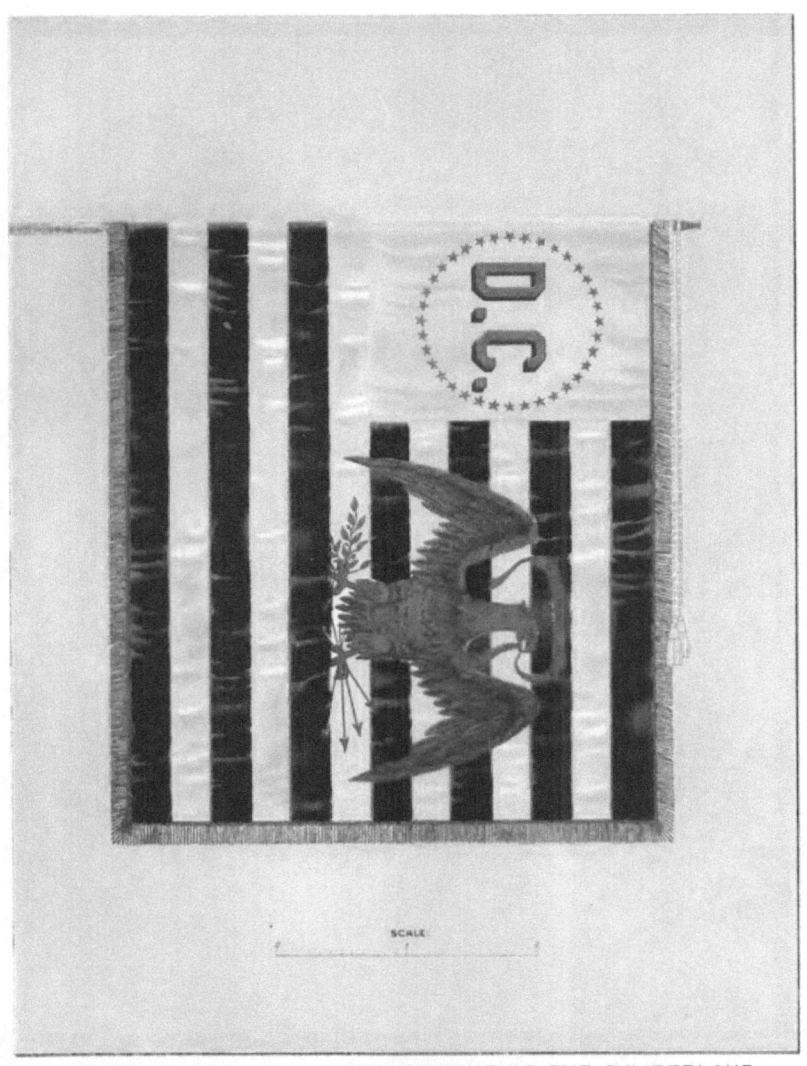

HEADQUARTERS OF THE DEPARTMENT OF THE CUMBERLAND.
USED BY GEN. GEORGE H. THOMAS.

HEADQUARTERS OF THE ARMY OF THE POTOMAC
USED FROM MAY 1864 PRIOR TO WHICH TIME THE NATIONAL FLAG WAS USED

ARMY OF THE TENNESSEE.

HEADQUARTERS OF THE ARMY OF THE OHIO.

HEADQUARTERS OF GEN. BURNSIDE'S COMMAND.

GEN. JOHN F. REYNOLD'S FLAG

GEN. AVERILL'S HEADQUARTERS FLAG

GEN. KILPATRICK'S FLAG.

9TH ARMY CORPS

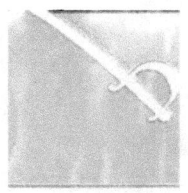

3

RESERVE CAVALRY BRIGADE   CAVALRY CORPS

ARTILLERY REGIMENTAL.

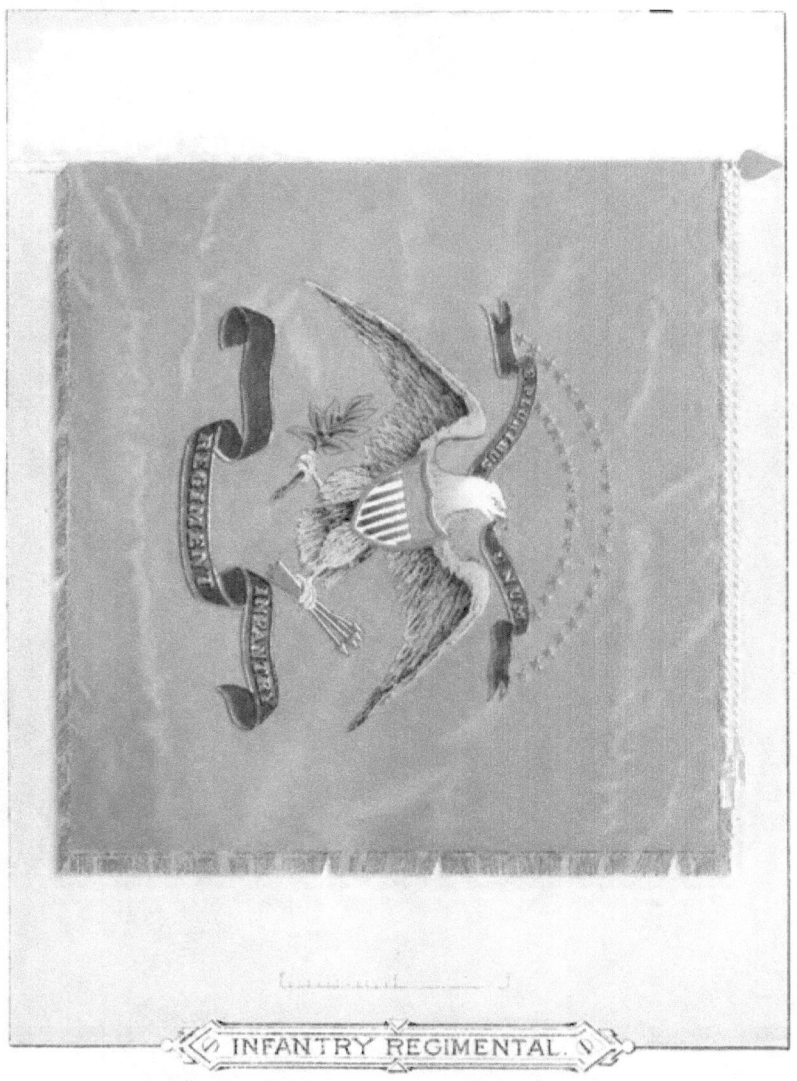

INFANTRY REGIMENTAL.

EACH REGIMENT OF INFANTRY CARRIED ALSO A SILK NATIONAL COLOR SIMILAR TO THE ARTILLERY NATIONAL (SHOWN ON PREVIOUS PAGE) EXCEPT THAT THE CORDS AND TASSELS WERE BLUE AND WHITE INTERMIXED, AND THAT THE INSCRIPTION INDICATED AN INFANTRY REGIMENT.

ALTHOUGH THE REGULATIONS OF 1863 PRESCRIBED WHITE STARS AND SILVER INSCRIPTIONS THE INFANTRY NATIONAL COLORS ACTUALLY CARRIED HAD GOLD STARS AND INSCRIPTIONS.

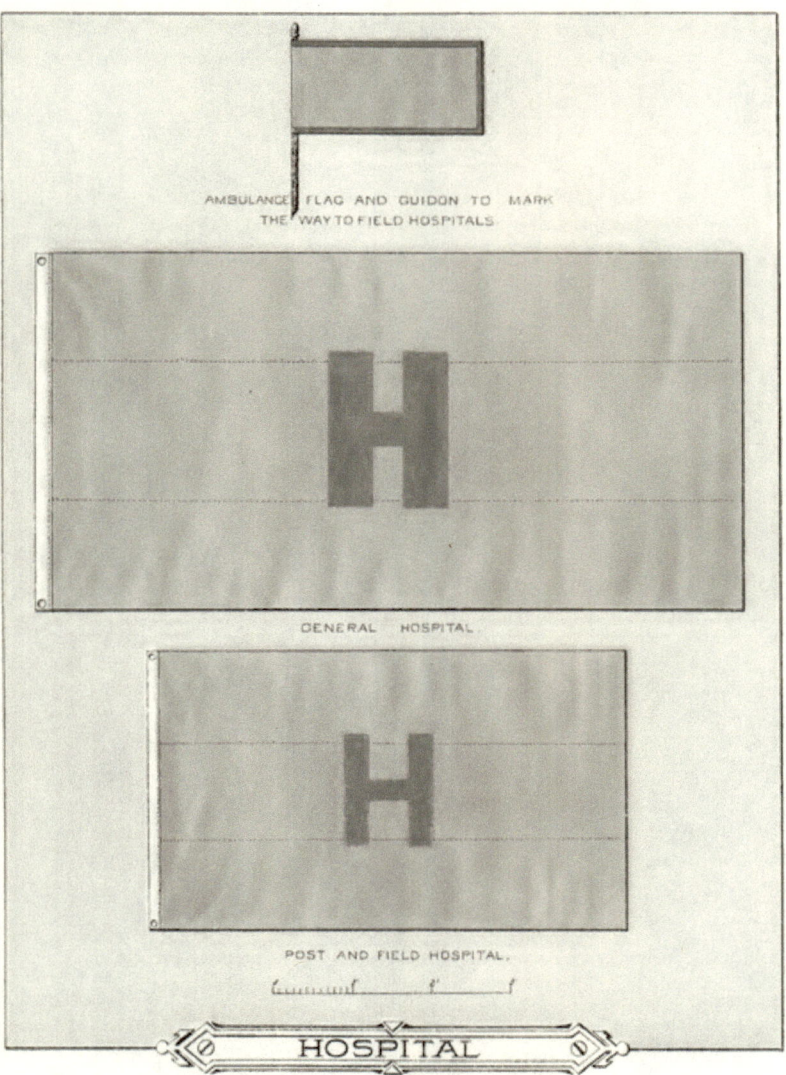

HEAD QUARTERS

ARTY. BRG.

CH'F Q.M.

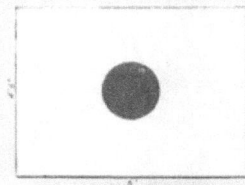
1st. DIV'N

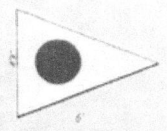
1st. BRG.

2nd. BRG.

4th BRG.

1ST ARMY CORPS.

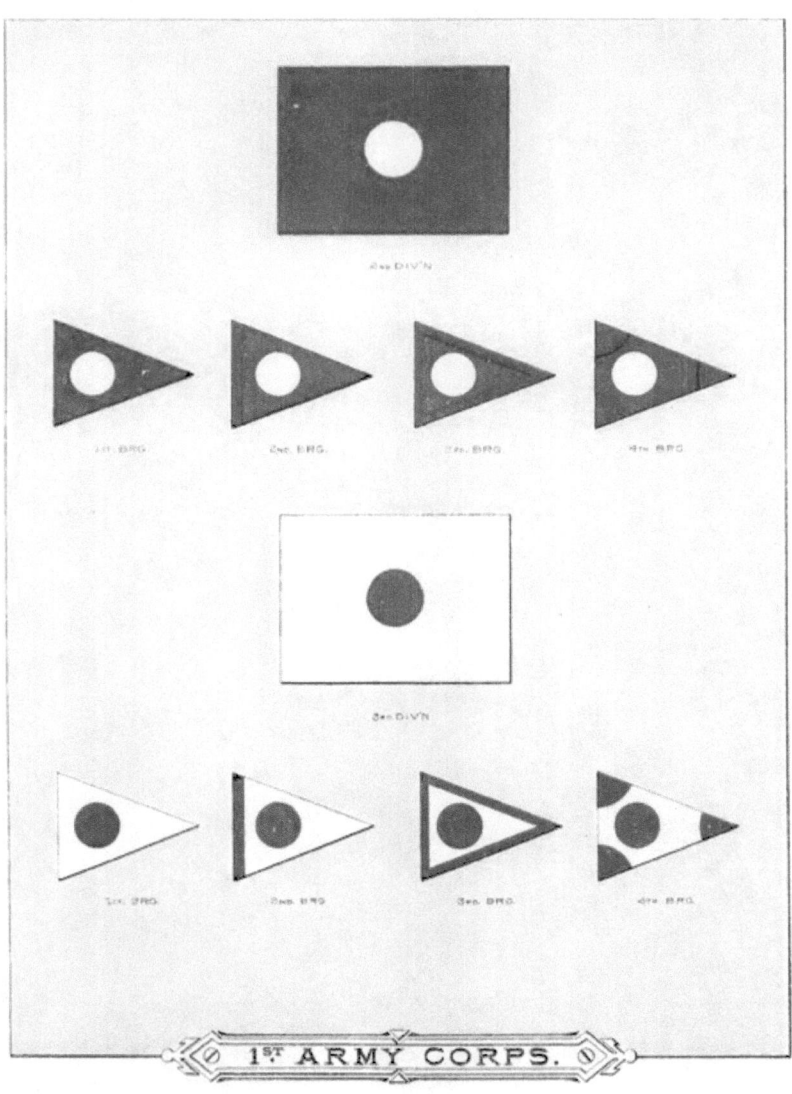

HEAD QUARTERS

ARTY BRG.

CH'F Q.M.

1st. DIV'N.

1st. BRG.

2nd. BRG.

3rd. BRG.

4th. BRG.

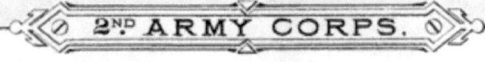

2ND ARMY CORPS.

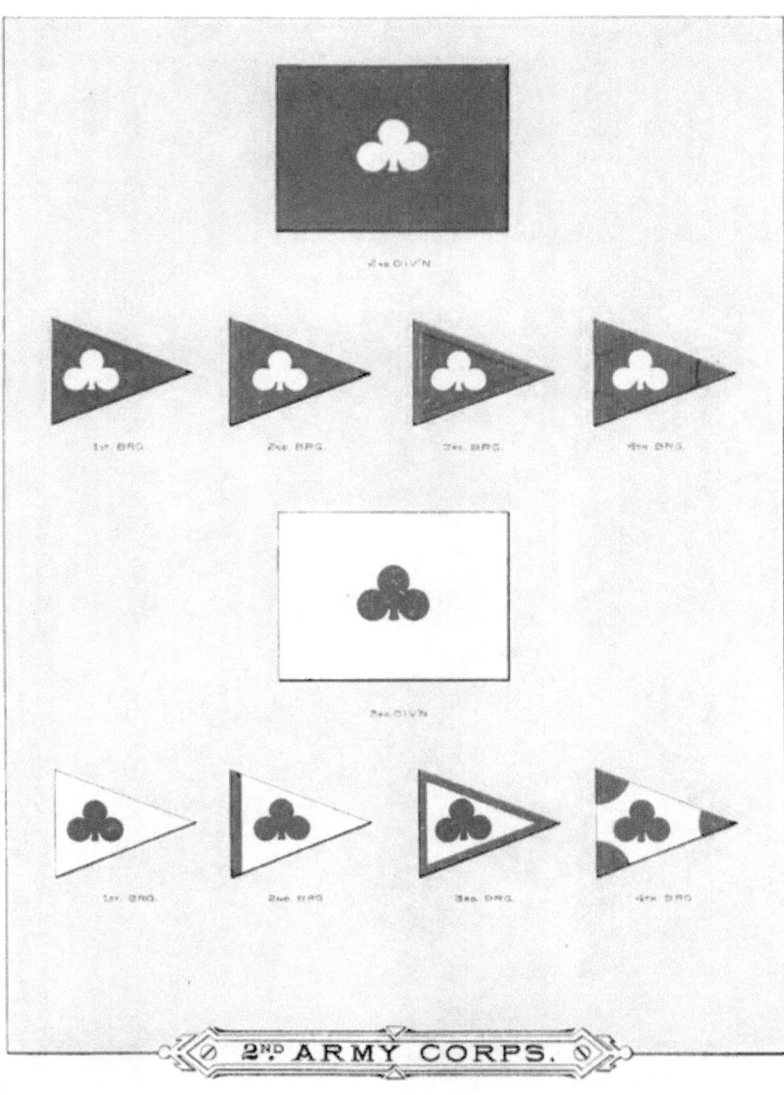

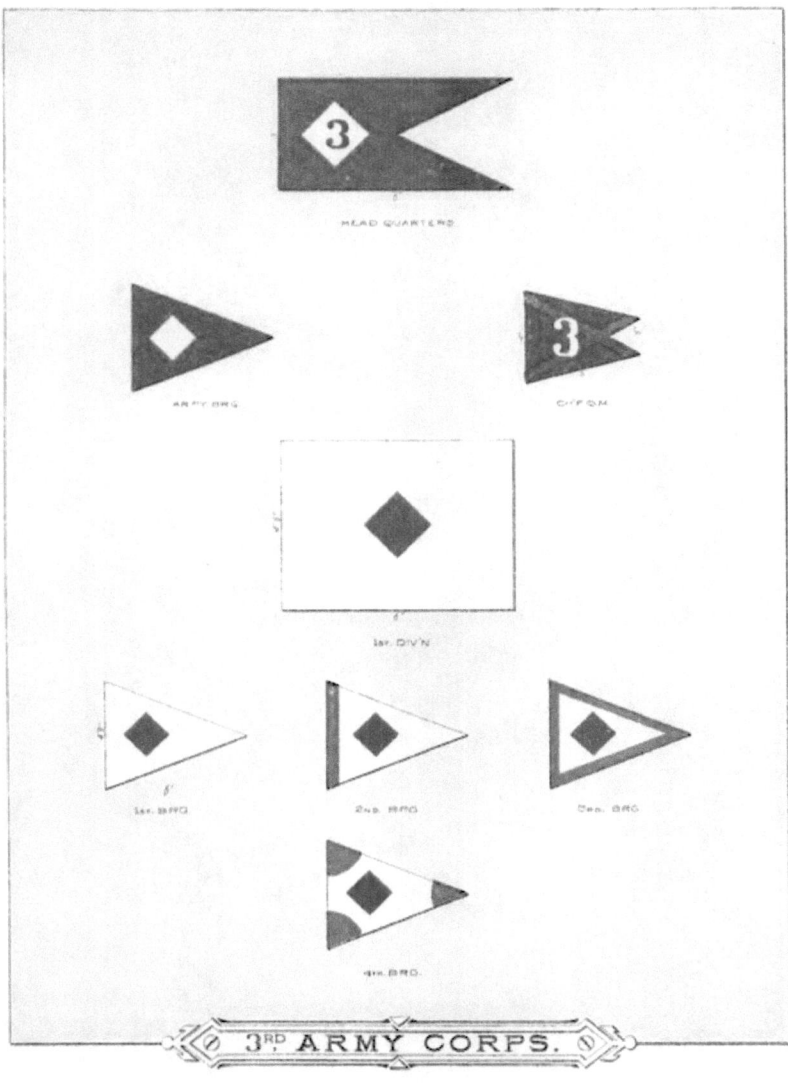

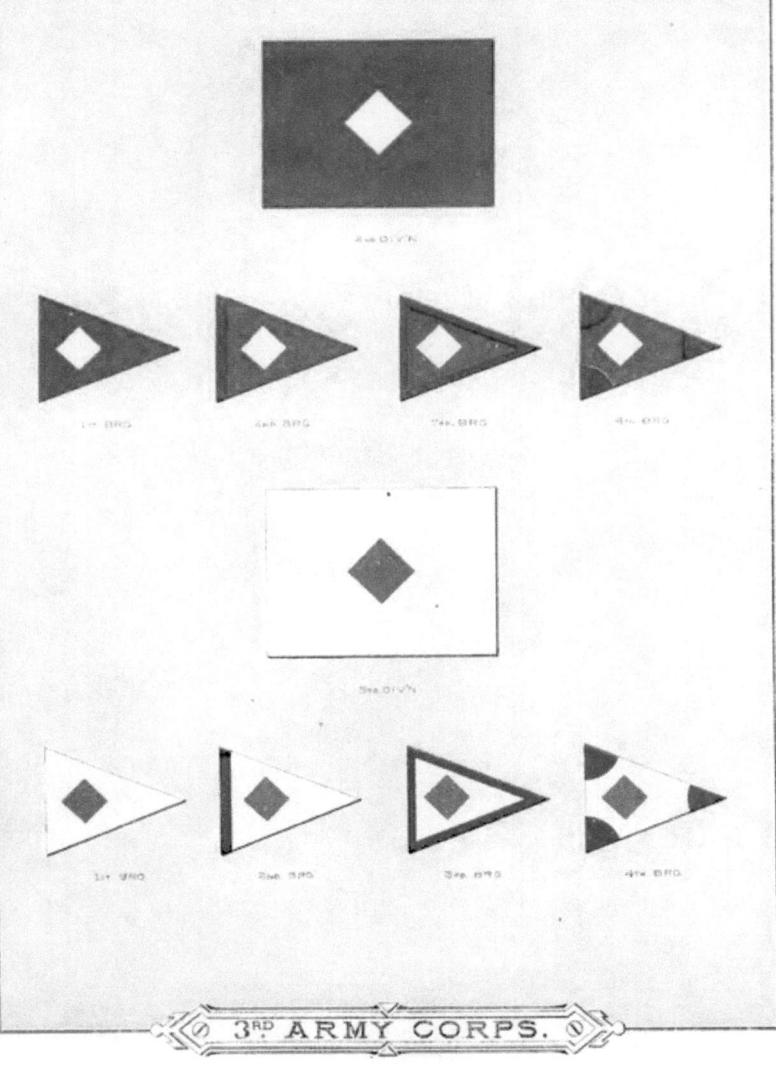

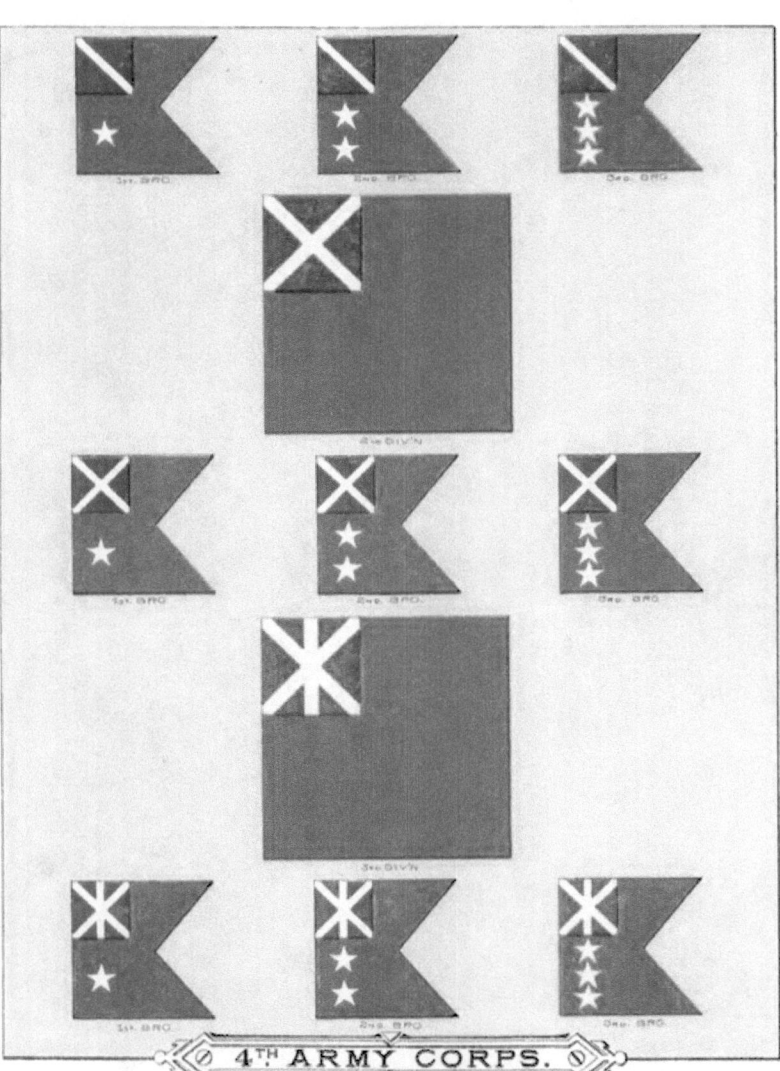

HEAD QUARTERS

ARTY BRIG.

CH'F Q.M.

1st. DIV'N.

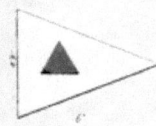
1st. BRG.

2nd. BRG.

3rd. BRG.

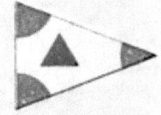
4th. BRG.

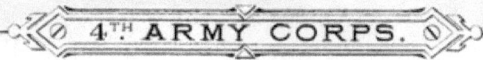
4TH ARMY CORPS.

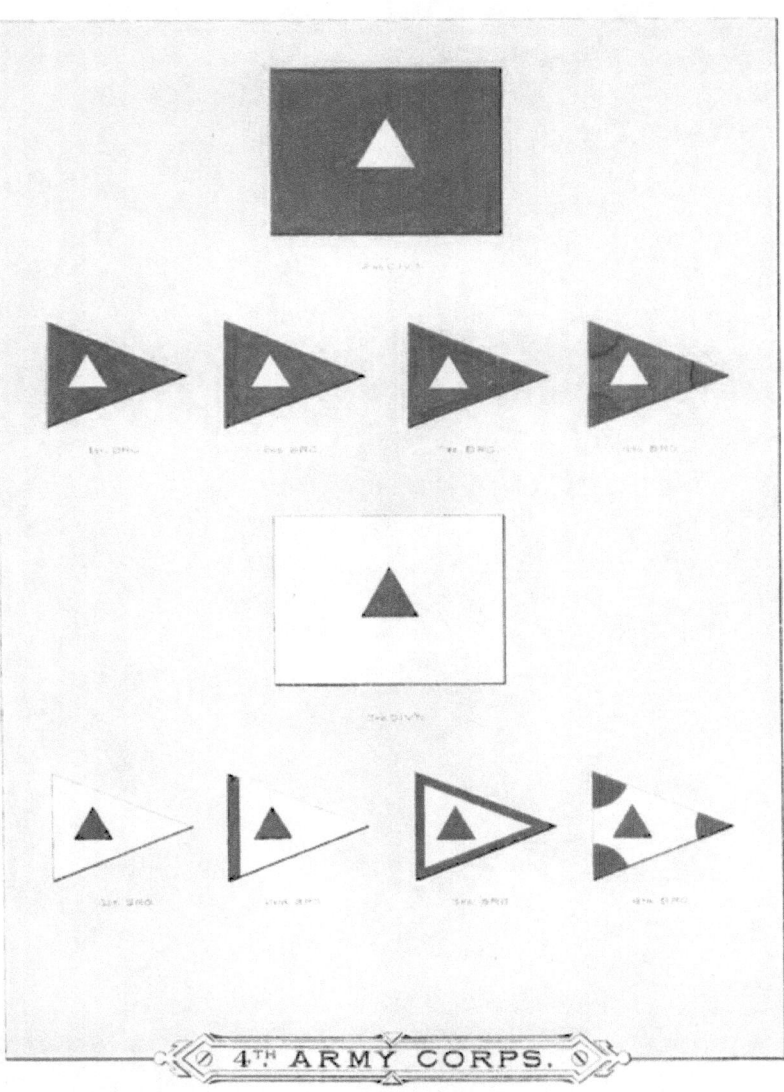

4TH ARMY CORPS.

HEAD QUARTERS.

ART'Y BRG.

CH F Q.M.

1ST DIV'N.

1ST BRG.

2ND BRG.

3RD BRG.

4TH BRG.

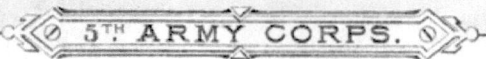
5TH ARMY CORPS.

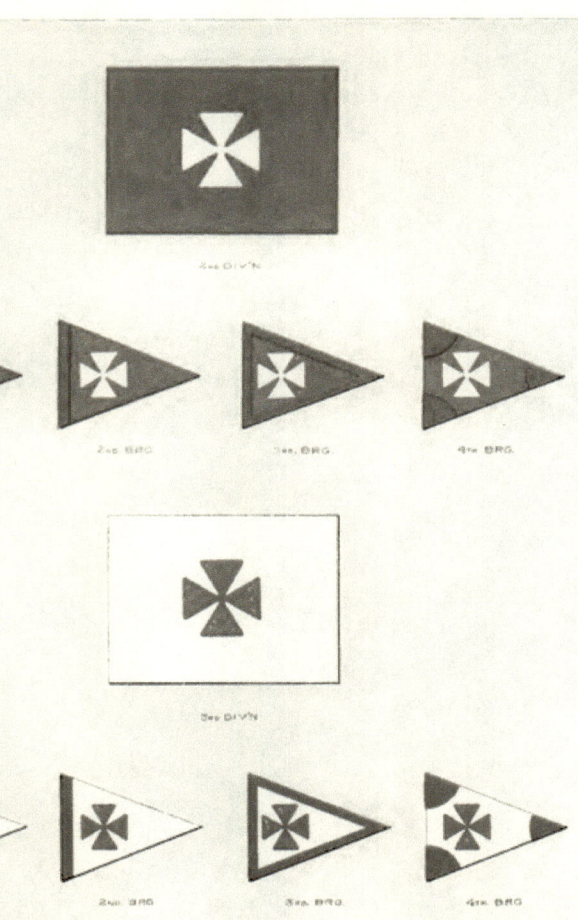

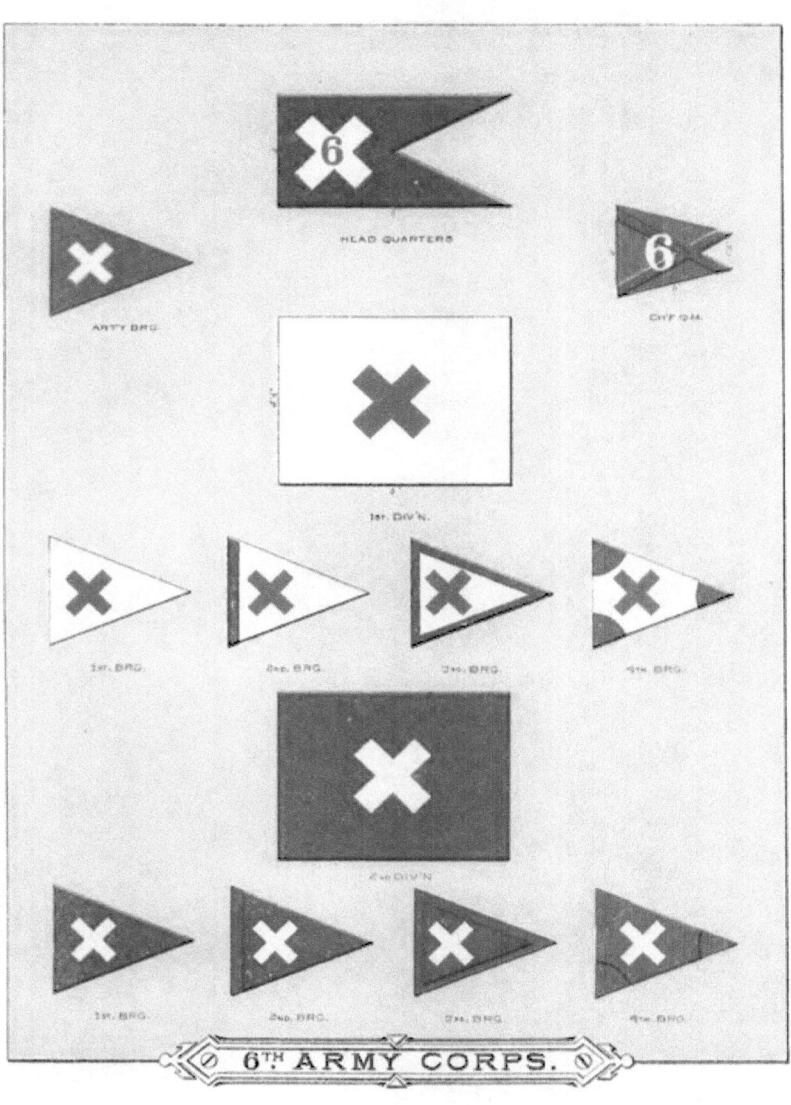

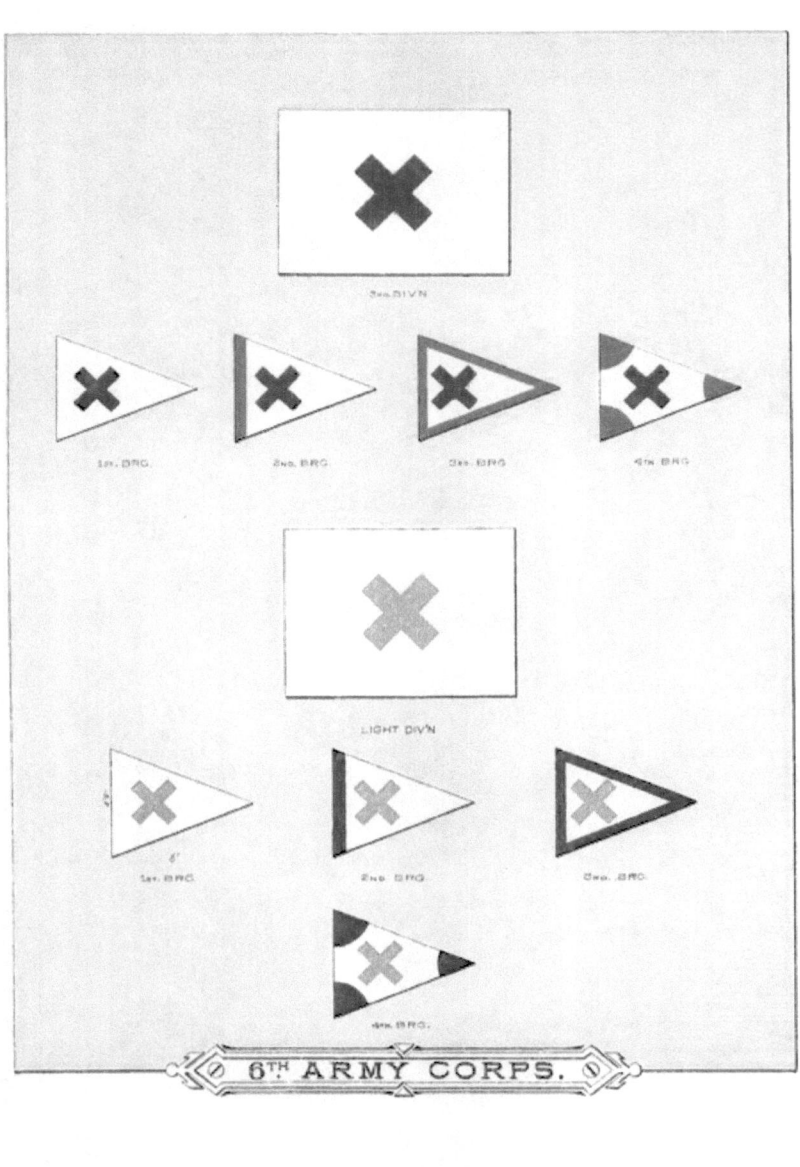

HEAD QUARTERS

ARTY. BRG.

CH'F Q.M.

1st. DIV'N

1st. BRG.   2nd. BRG.   3rd. BRG.

4th. BRG.

7TH ARMY CORPS.

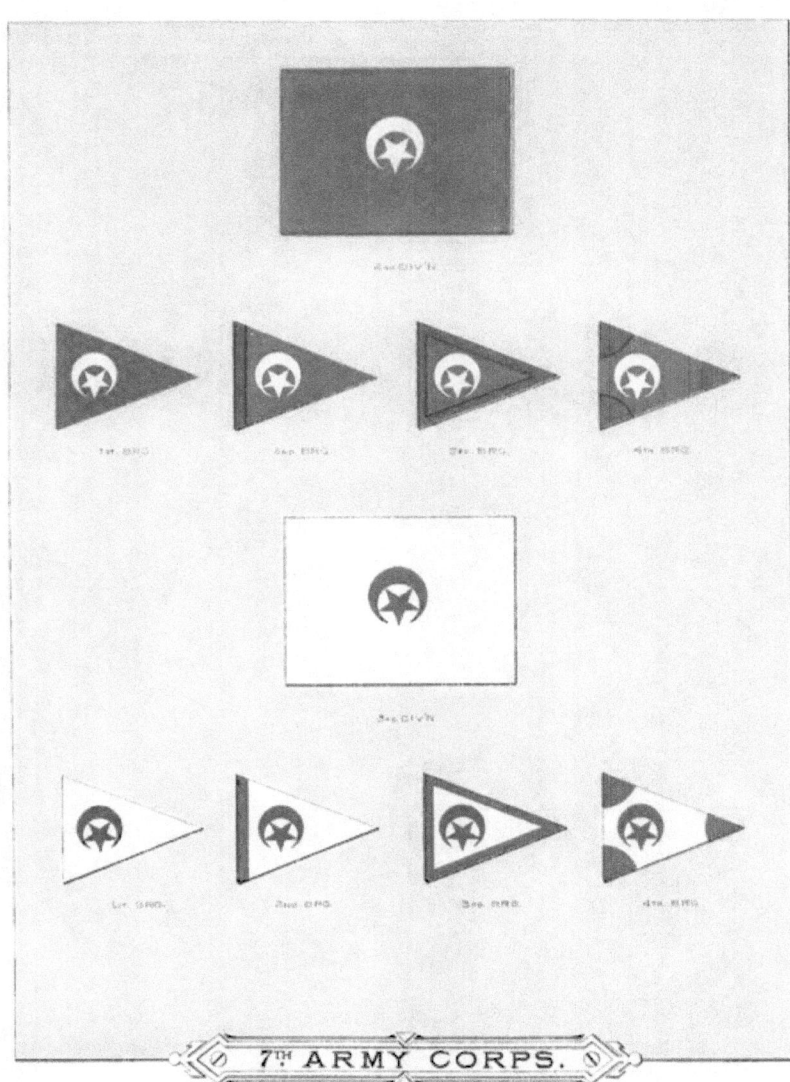

HEAD QUARTERS

ART'Y BRG.

CH'F Q.M.

1st DIV'N.

1st BRG.

2nd BRG.

3rd BRG.

4th BRG.

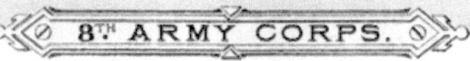
8TH ARMY CORPS.

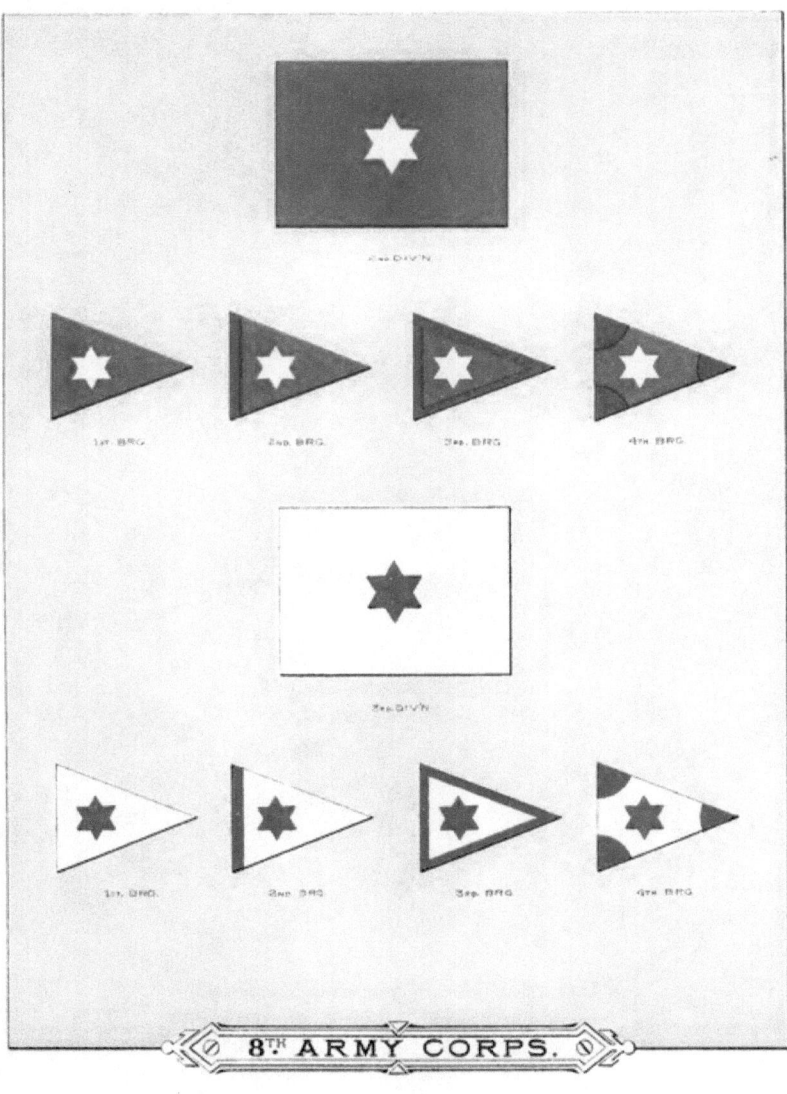

8TH ARMY CORPS.

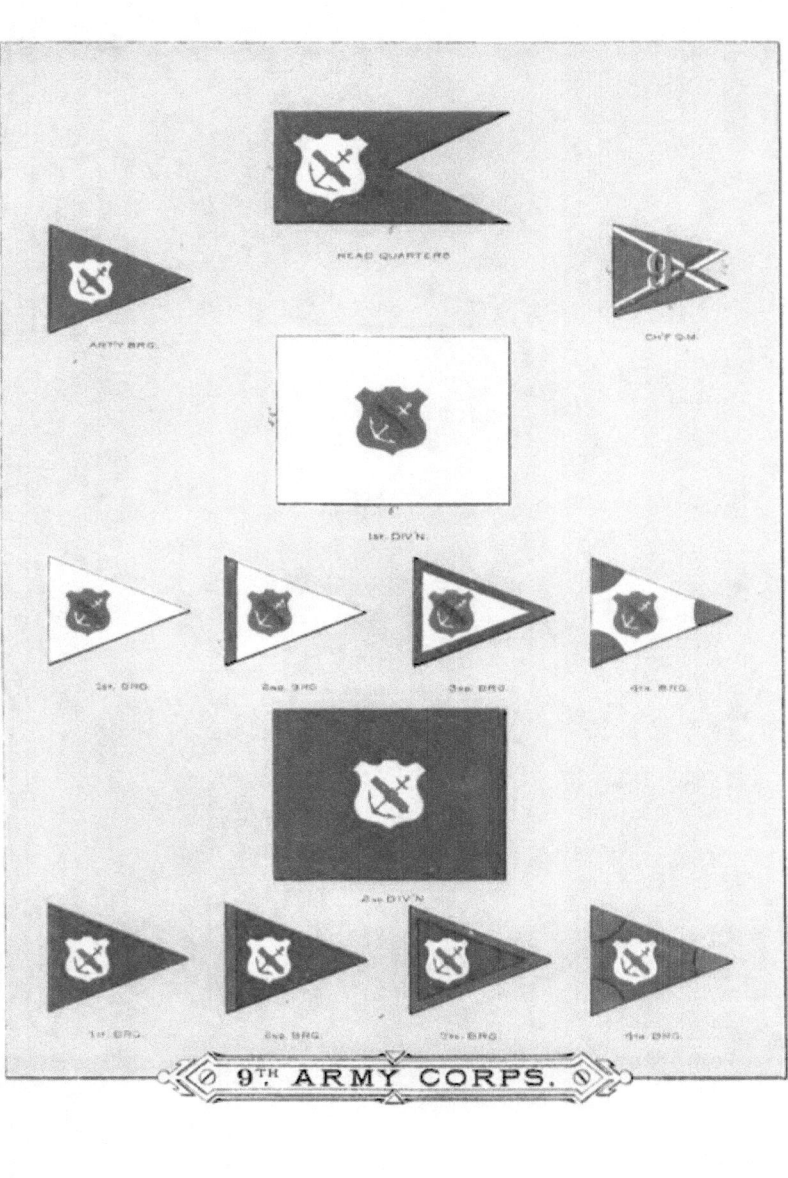

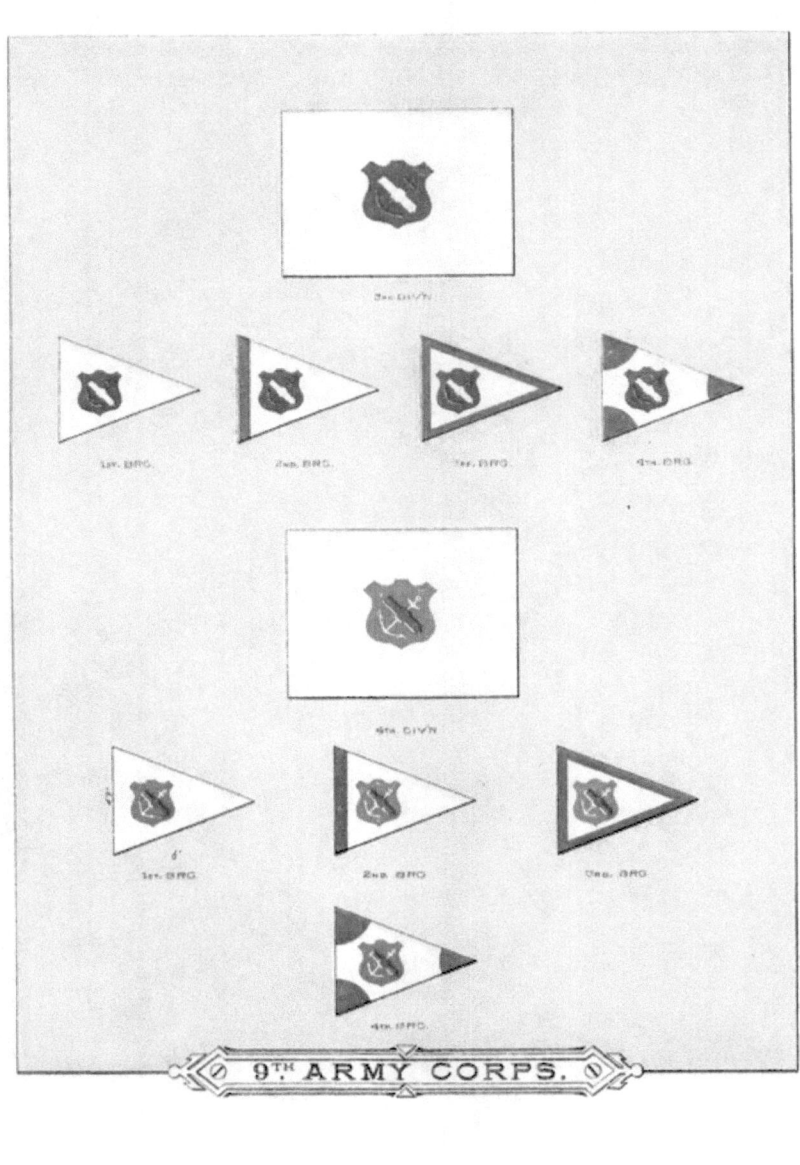

HEAD QUARTERS.

ART'Y BRG.

CH.F Q.M.

1st. DIV'N

1st. BRG.

2nd. BRG.

3rd. BRG.

10TH ARMY CORPS.

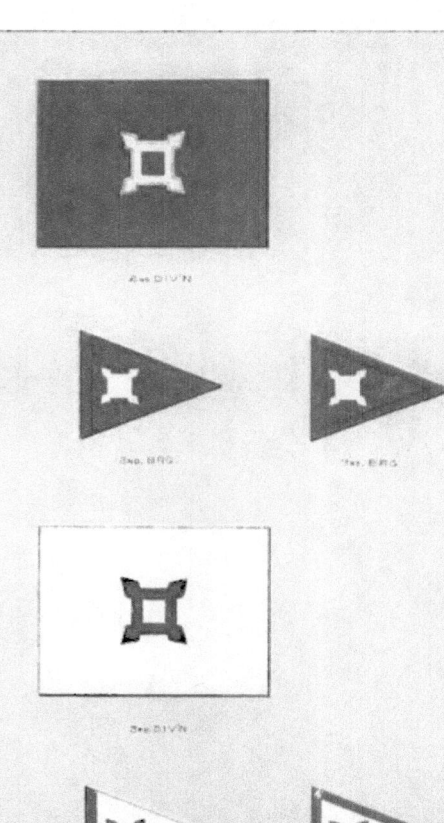

HEAD QUARTERS

ARTY BRG

1st DIV'N

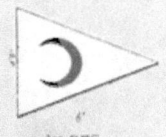
1st BRG.

CH'F Q.M.

4th BRG.

11TH ARMY CORPS.

2nd DIV'N

1st. BRG.　　2nd. BRG.　　3rd. BRG.　　4th. BRG.

3rd DIV'N

1st. BRG.　　2nd. BRG.　　3rd. BRG.　　4th. BRG.

11TH ARMY CORPS.

HEAD QUARTERS

CH'F S.M.

ART'Y BRG.

12TH ARMY CORPS.

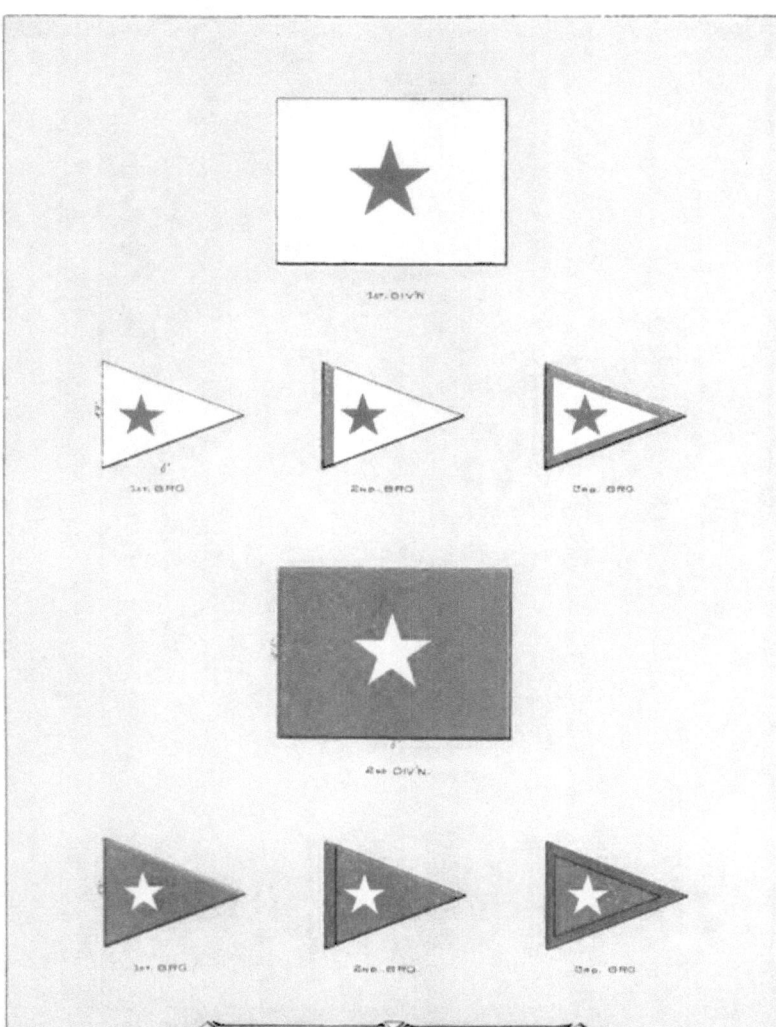

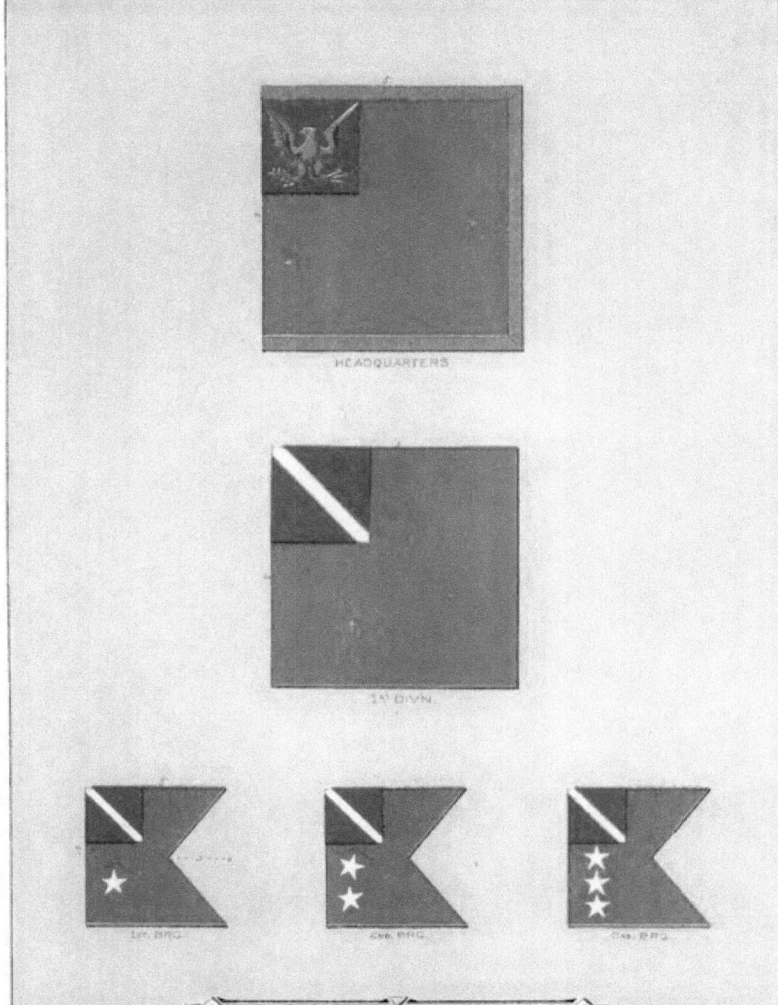

2nd DIV'N

1st. BRG.

2nd. BRG.

3rd. BRG.

3rd DIV'N

1st. BRG.

2nd. BRG.

3rd. BRG.

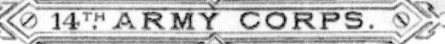

14TH ARMY CORPS.
DEPARTMENT OF THE CUMBERLAND

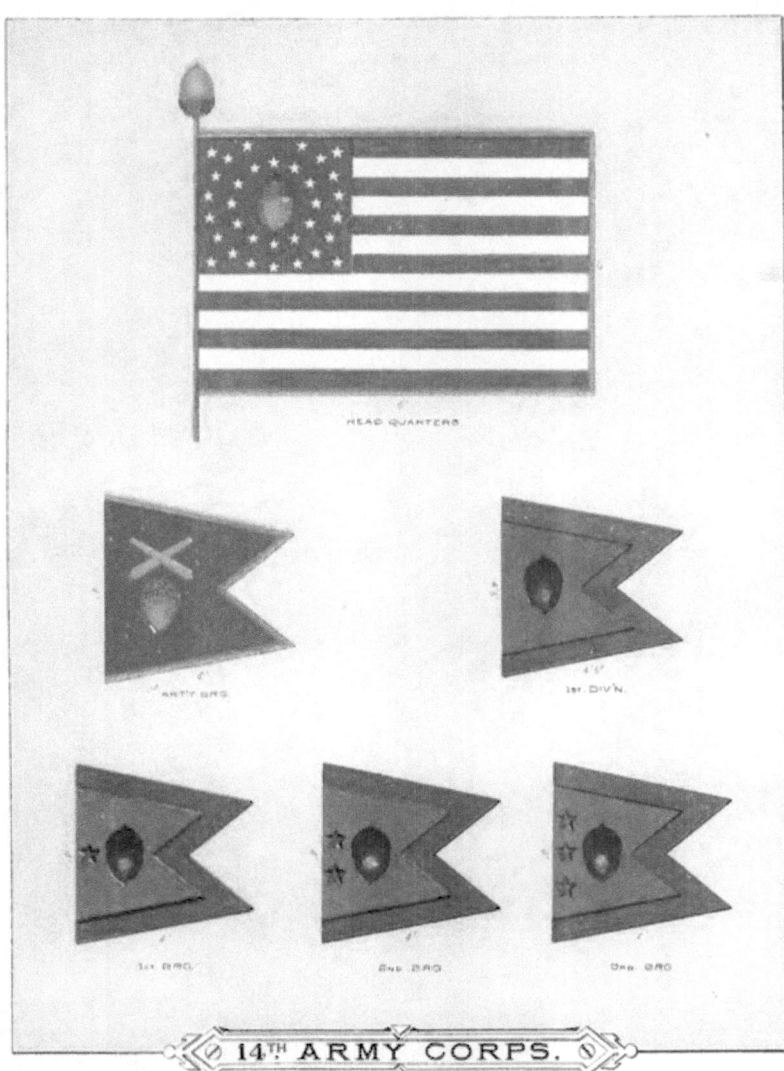

14TH ARMY CORPS.

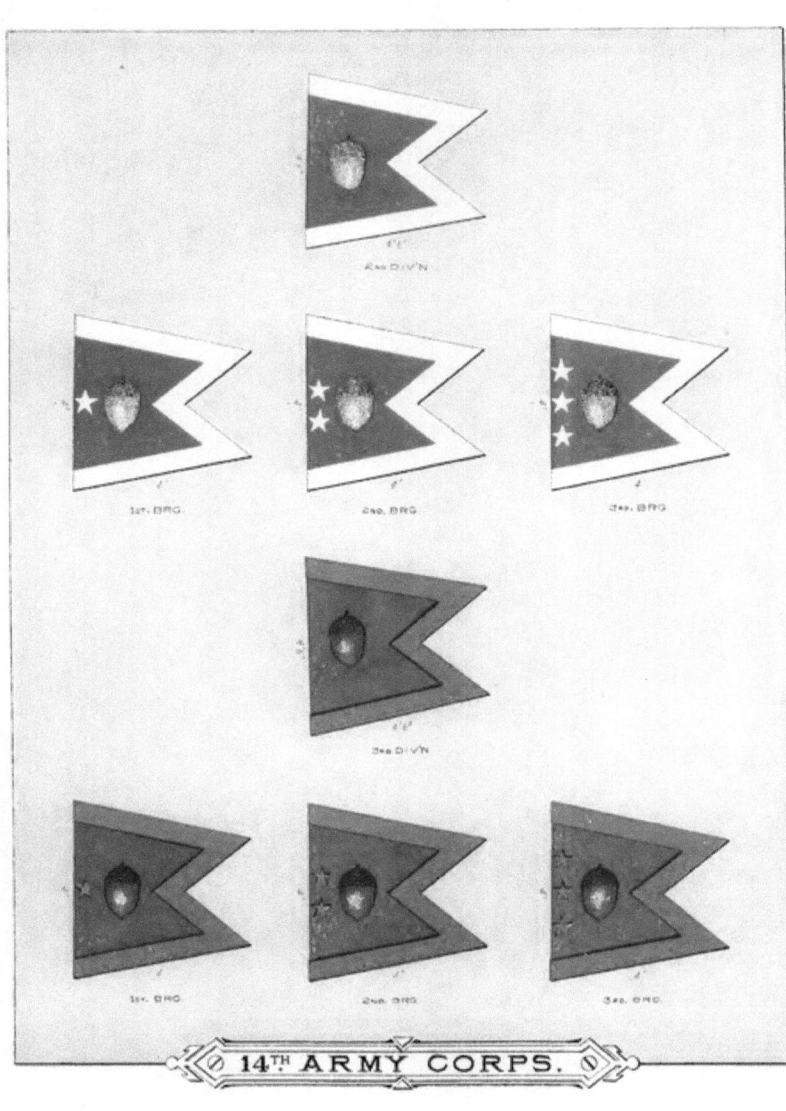

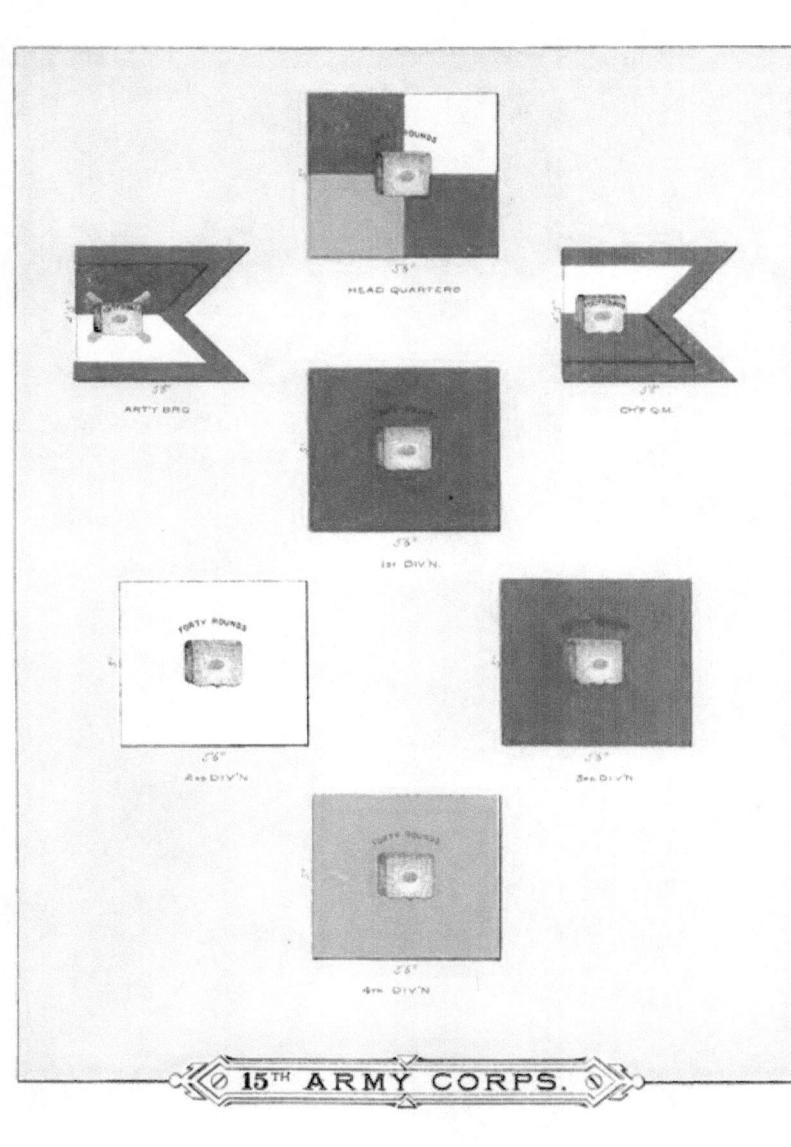

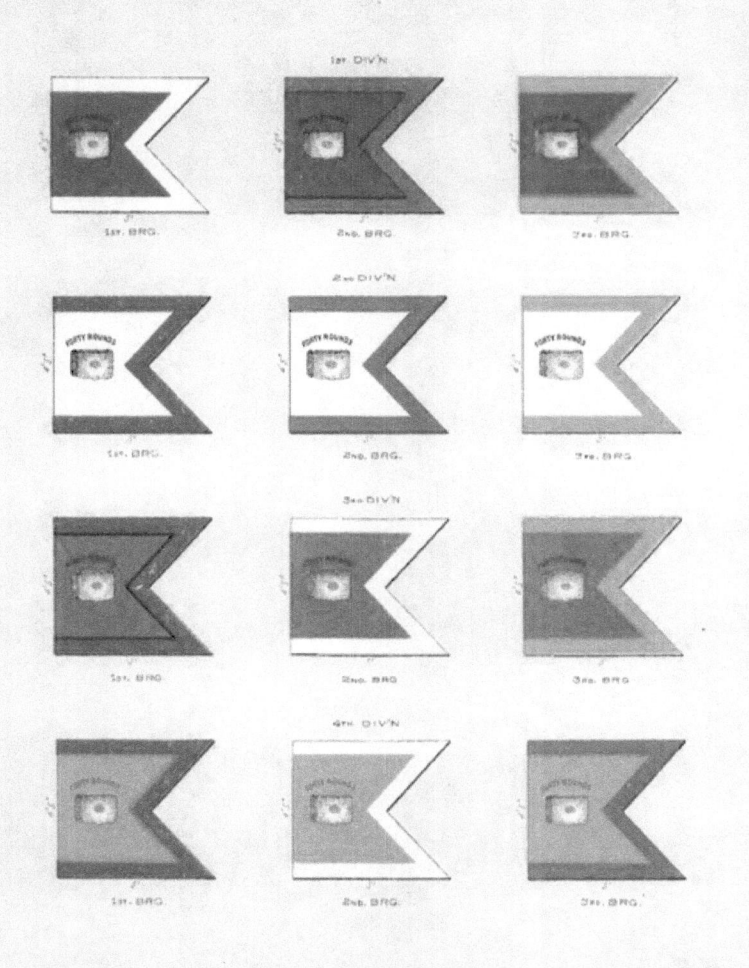

HEAD QUARTERS

ARTY. BRG.

CH'F Q.M.

1st. DIV'N.

1st. BRG.

2nd. BRG.

3rd. BRG.

4th. BRG.

16TH ARMY CORPS.

2nd DIV'N

1st. BRG.   2nd. BRG.   3rd. BRG.   4th. BRG.

3rd DIV'N

1st. BRG.   2nd. BRG.   3rd. BRG.   4th. BRG.

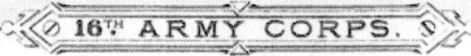
16TH ARMY CORPS.

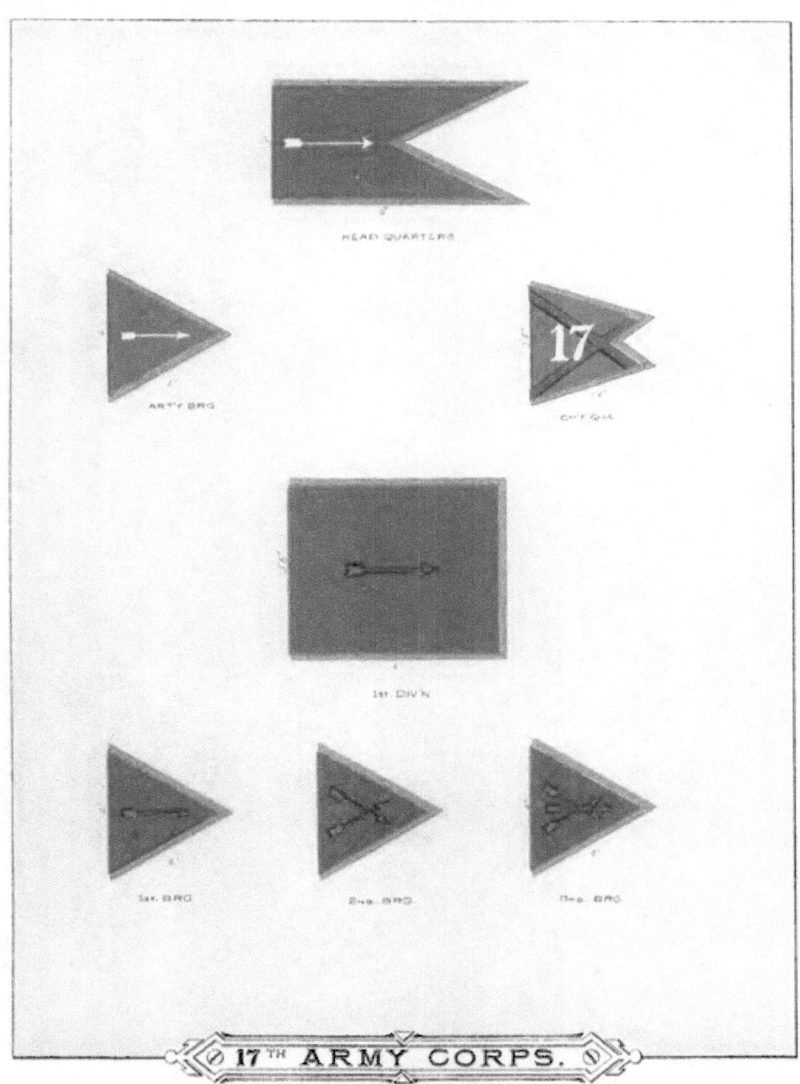

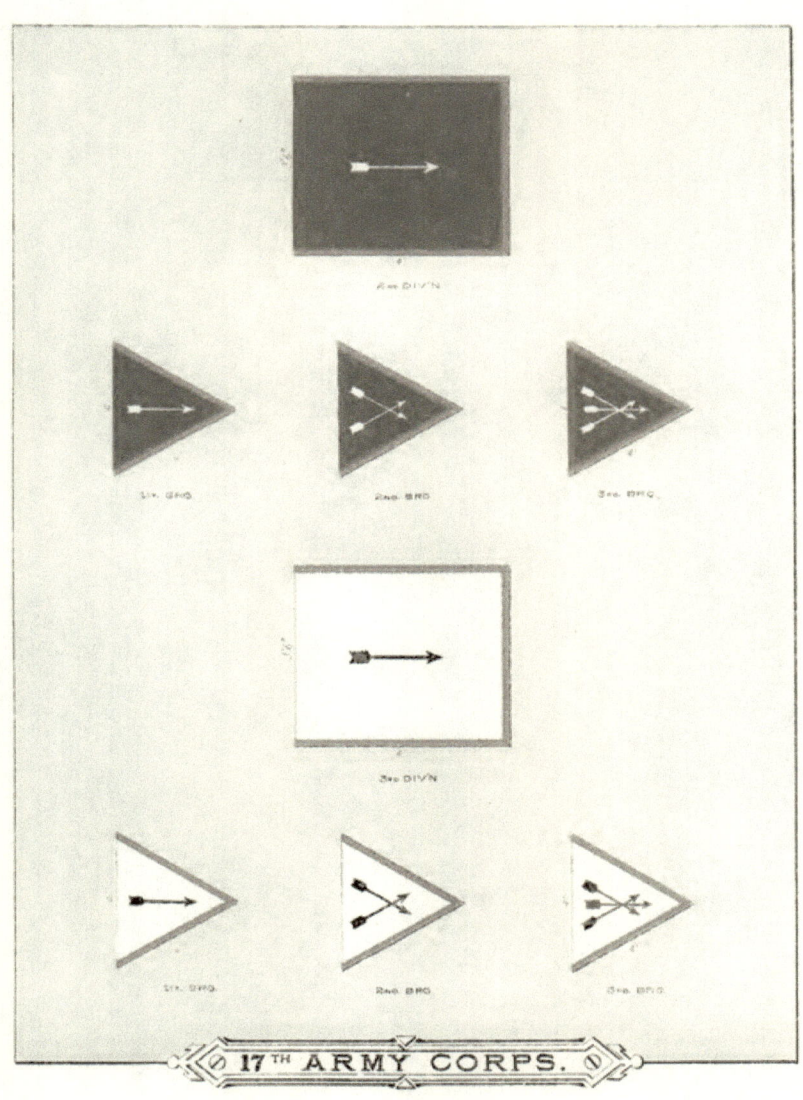

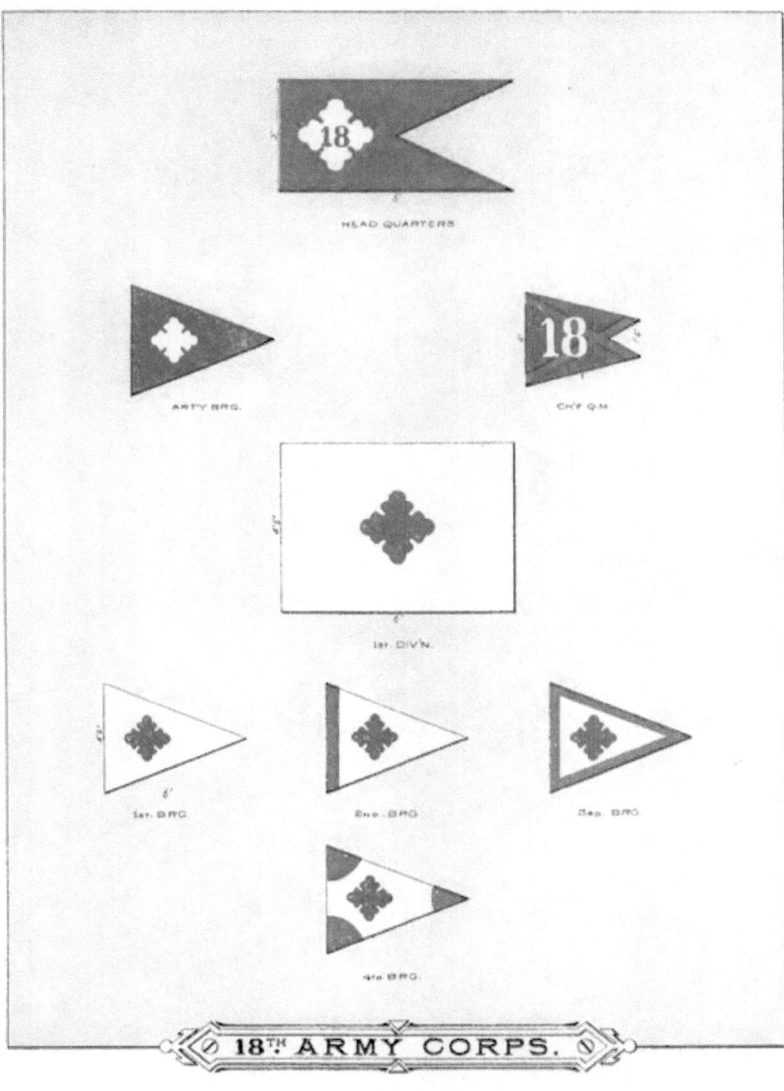

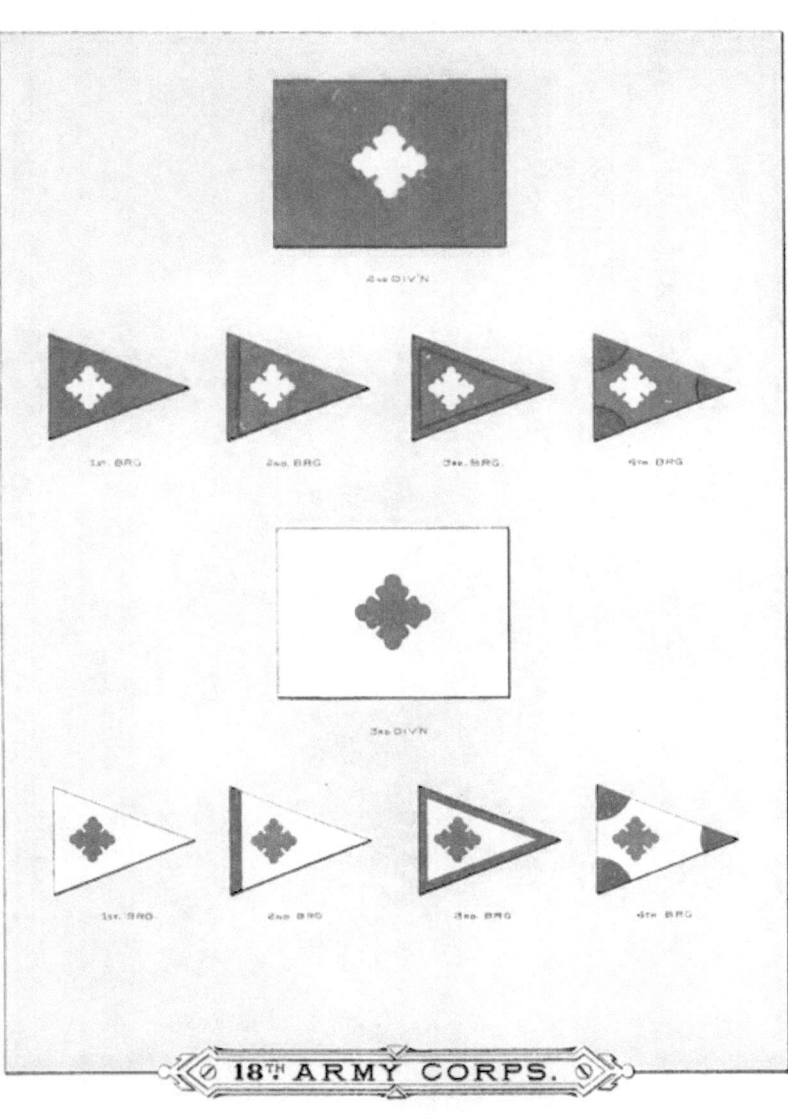

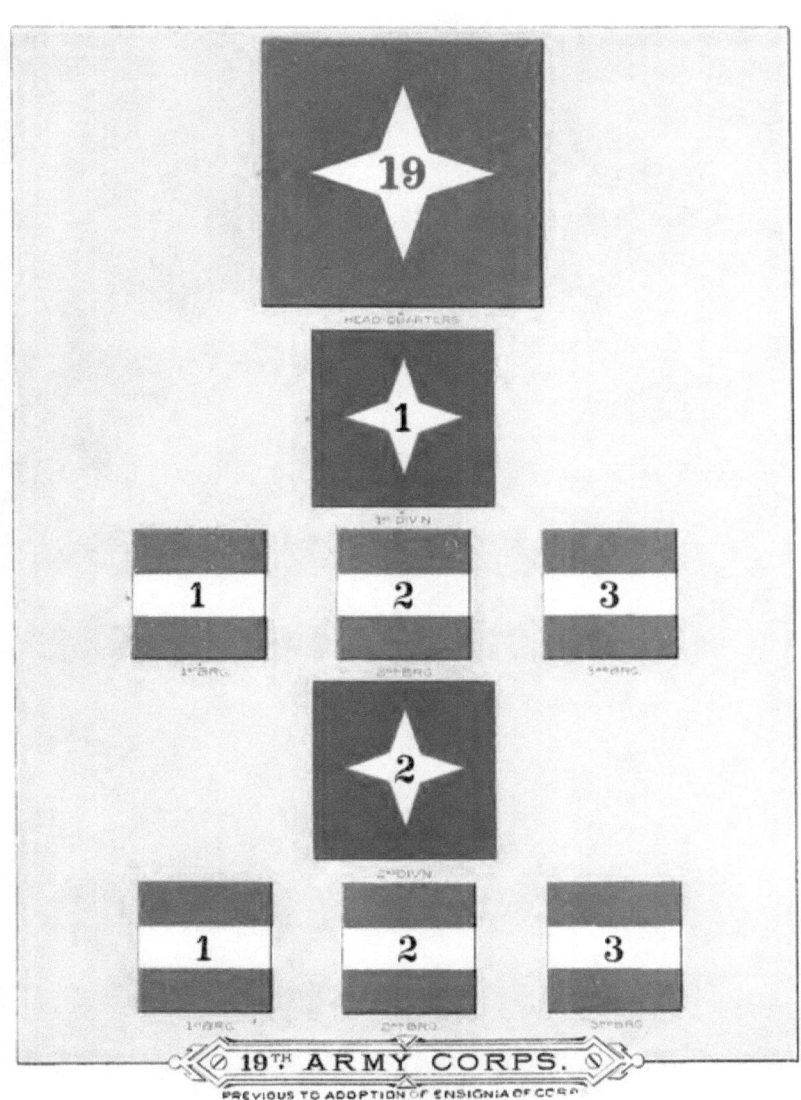

3RD DIVN

1ST BRG.   2ND BRG.   3RD BRG.

4TH DIVN

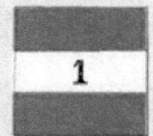 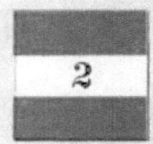 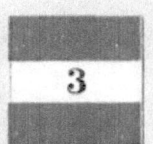
1ST BRG.   2ND BRG.   3RD BRG.

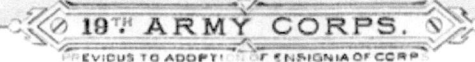

19TH ARMY CORPS.
PREVIOUS TO ADOPTION OF ENSIGNIA OF CORPS
G. O. N° 17 FEB. 18TH 1863

HEAD QUARTERS

ARTY BRG

CH'F Q.M.

1st DIV'N

1st BRG.

2nd BRG.

3rd BRG.

4th BRG.

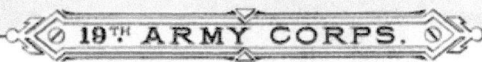

19TH ARMY CORPS.

2ND DIV'N

1ST. BRG.   2ND. BRG.   3RD. BRG.   4TH. BRG.

3RD DIV'N

1ST. BRG.   2ND. BRG.   3RD. BRG.   4TH. BRG.

19TH ARMY CORPS.

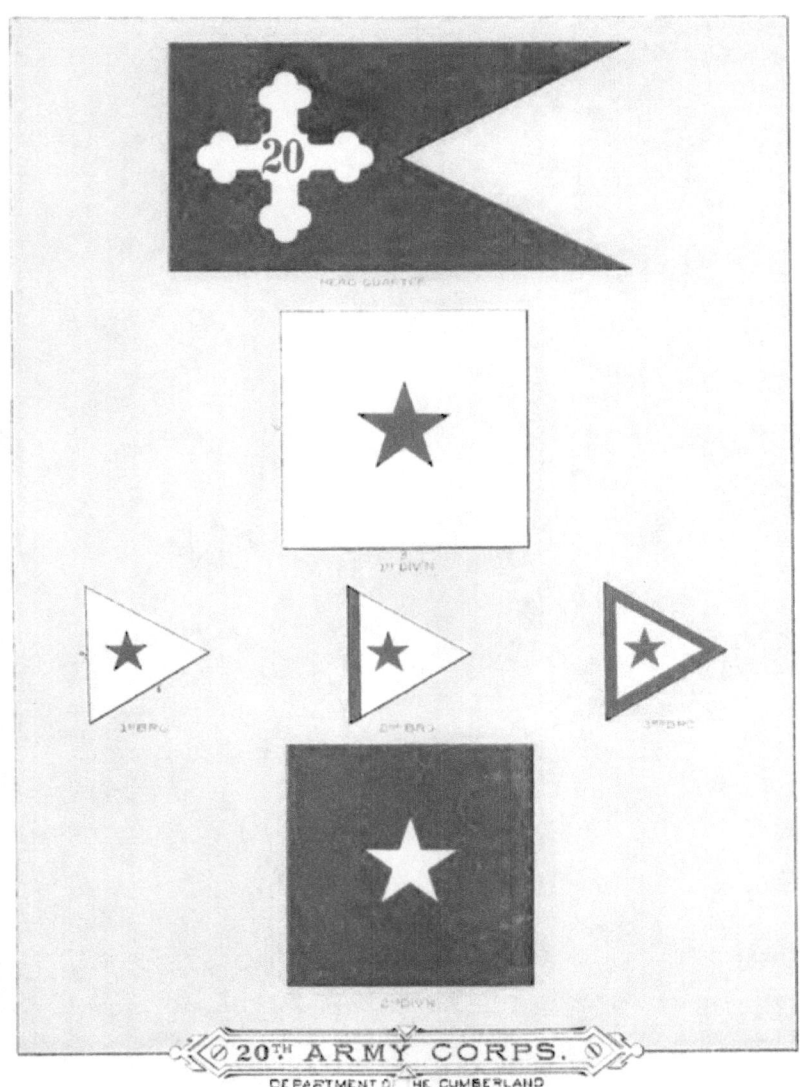

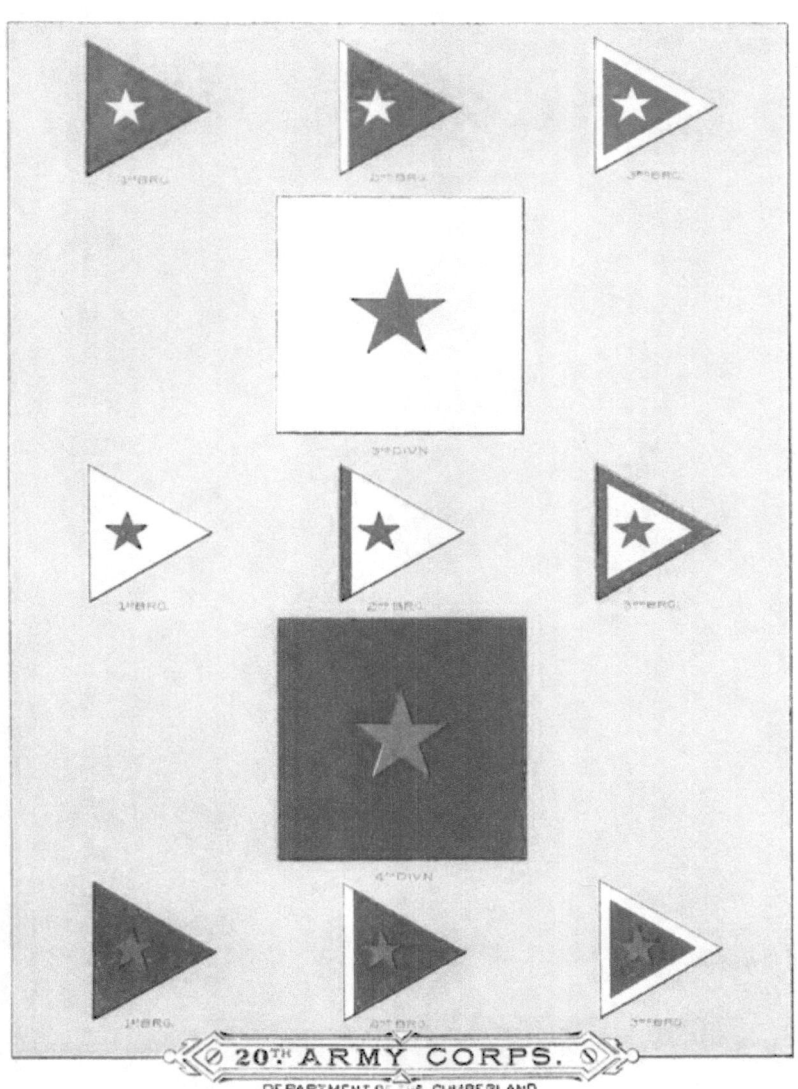

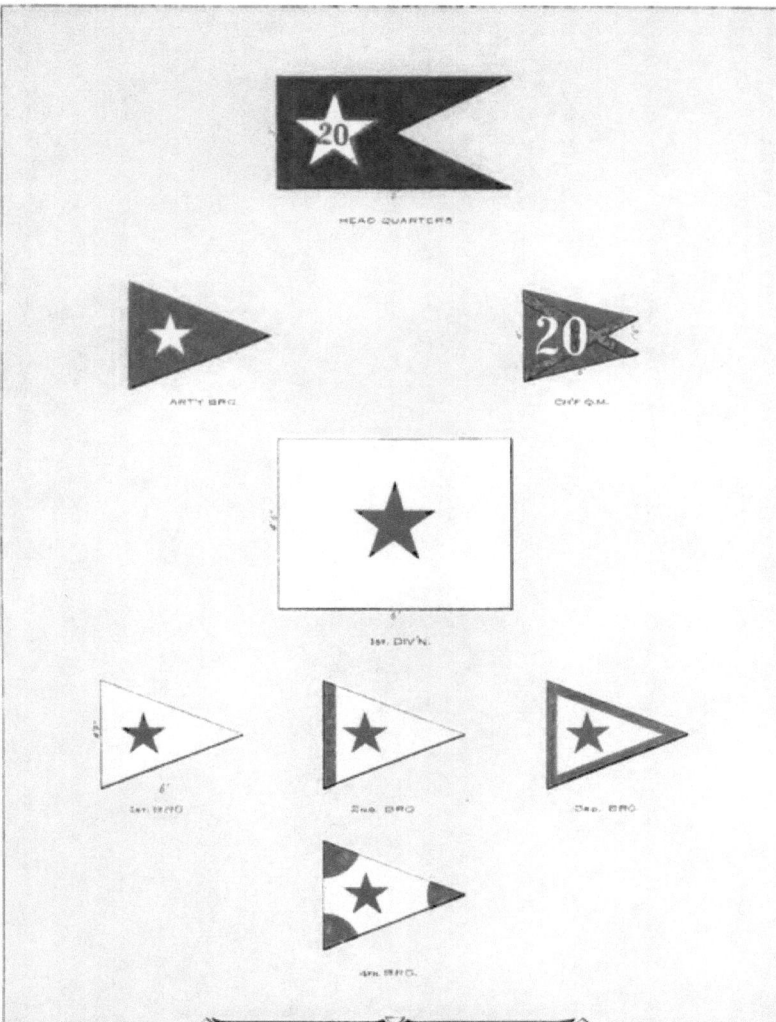

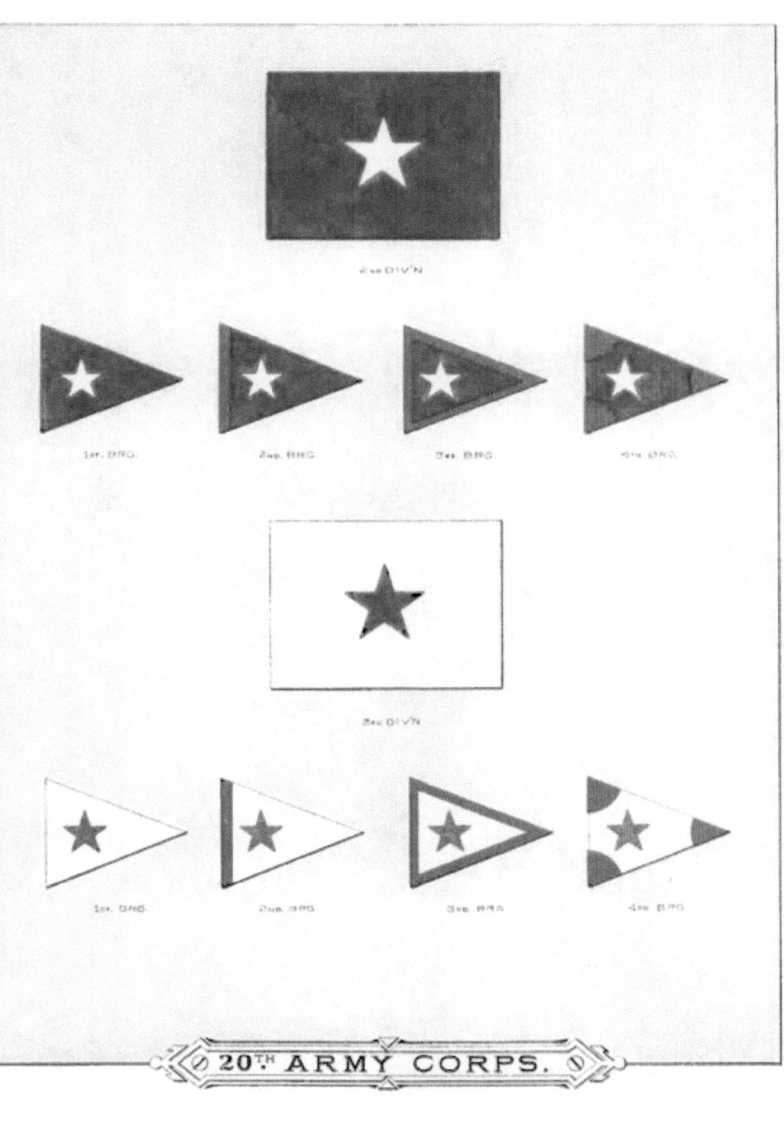

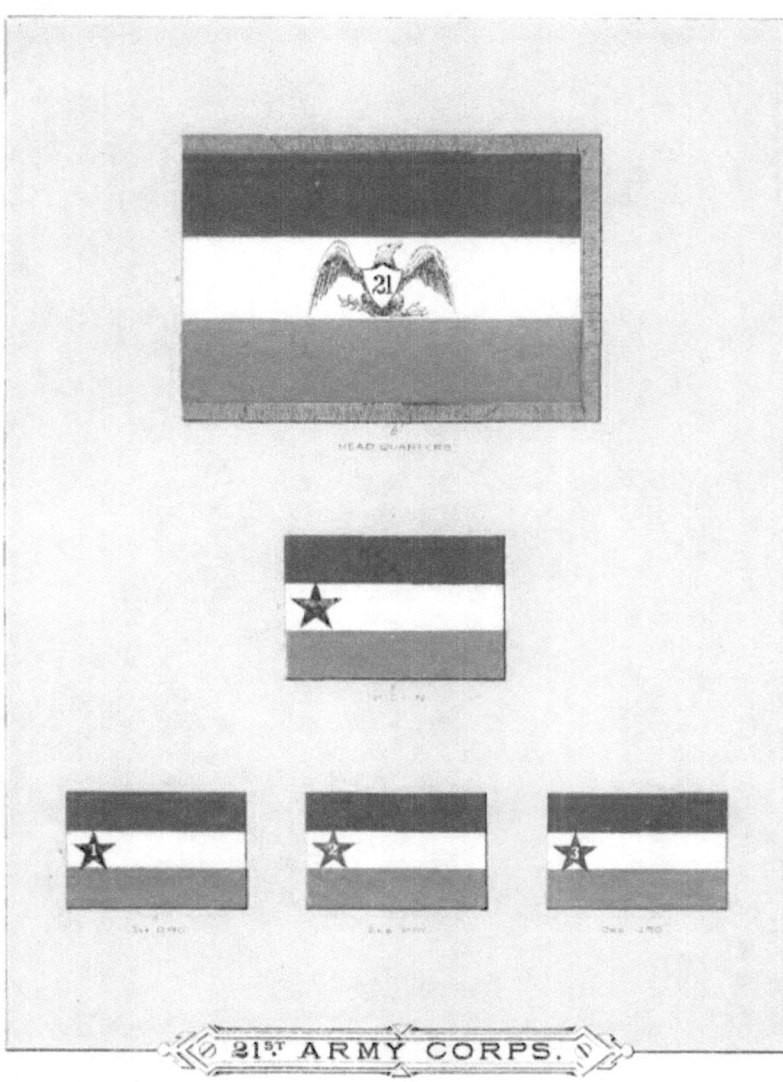

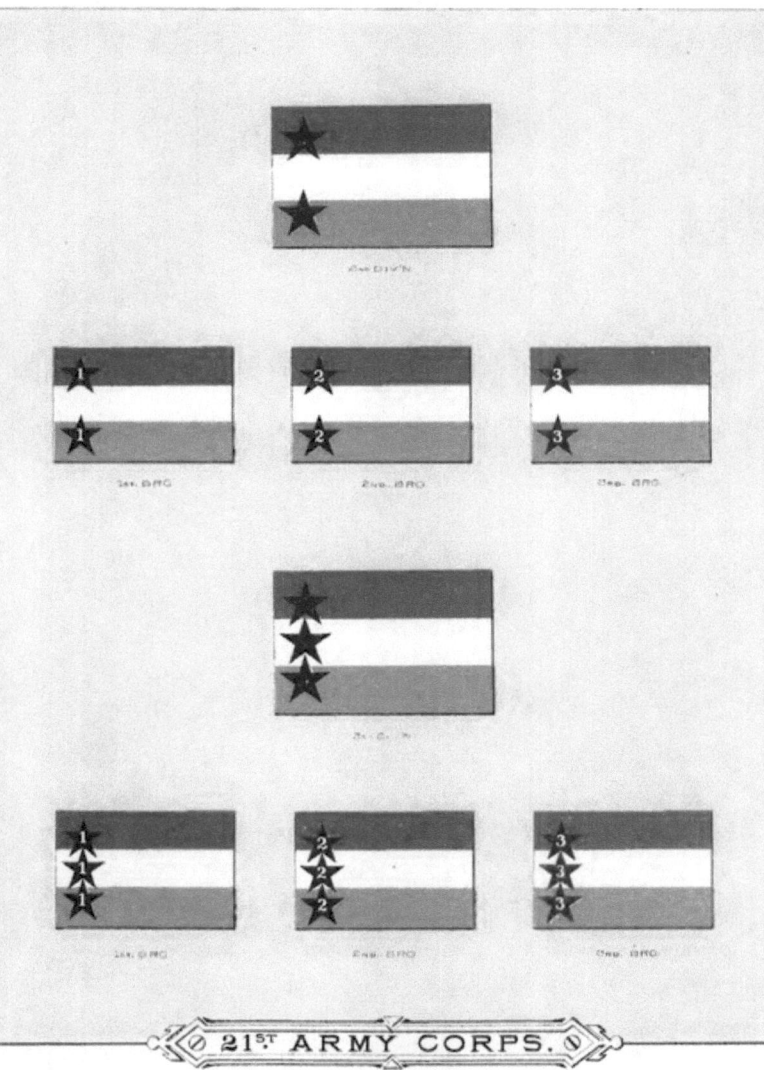

HEAD QUARTERS

ARTY BRG

CH F Q M

1st DIV'N.

1st BRG

2nd BRG

3rd BRG

4th BRG

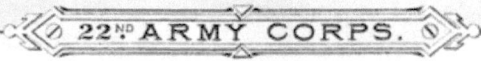
22ND ARMY CORPS.

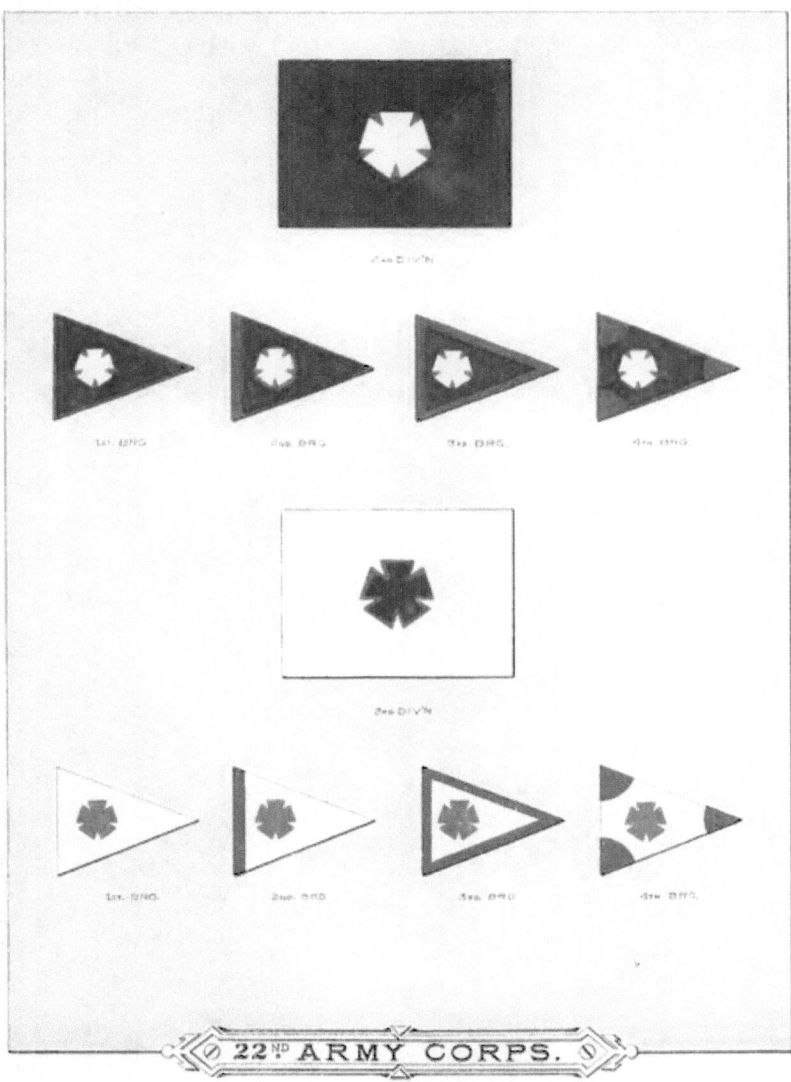

HEADQUARTERS

1st. DIV'N

1st. BRG.

2nd. BRG.

3rd. BRG.

23RD ARMY CORPS.

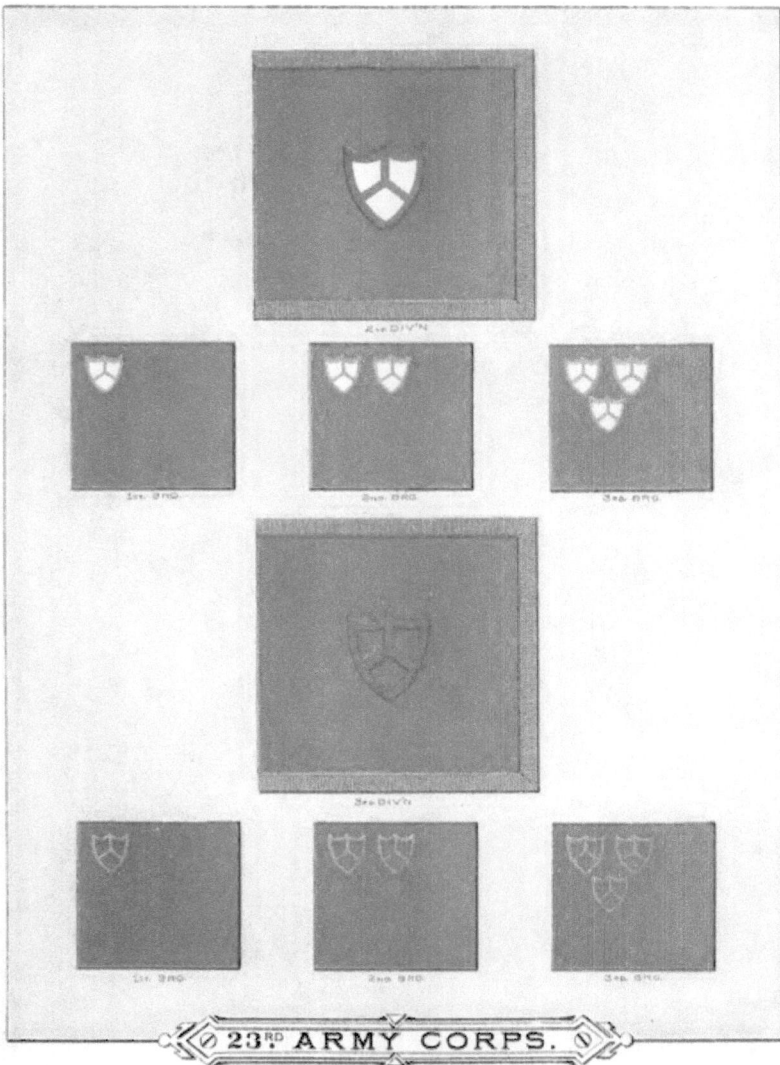

HEAD QUARTERS

ARTY. BRG.   CH'F Q.M.

1st. DIV'N

1st. BRG.   2nd. BRG.   3rd. BRG.

4th. BRG.

24TH ARMY CORPS.

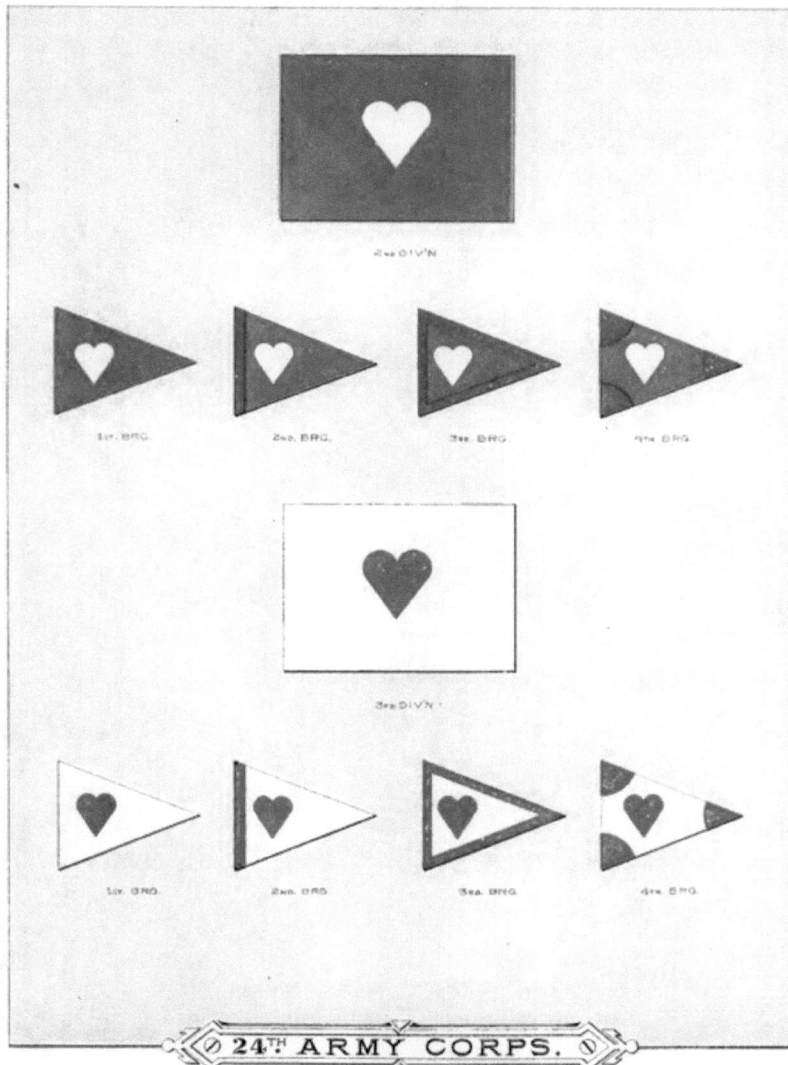

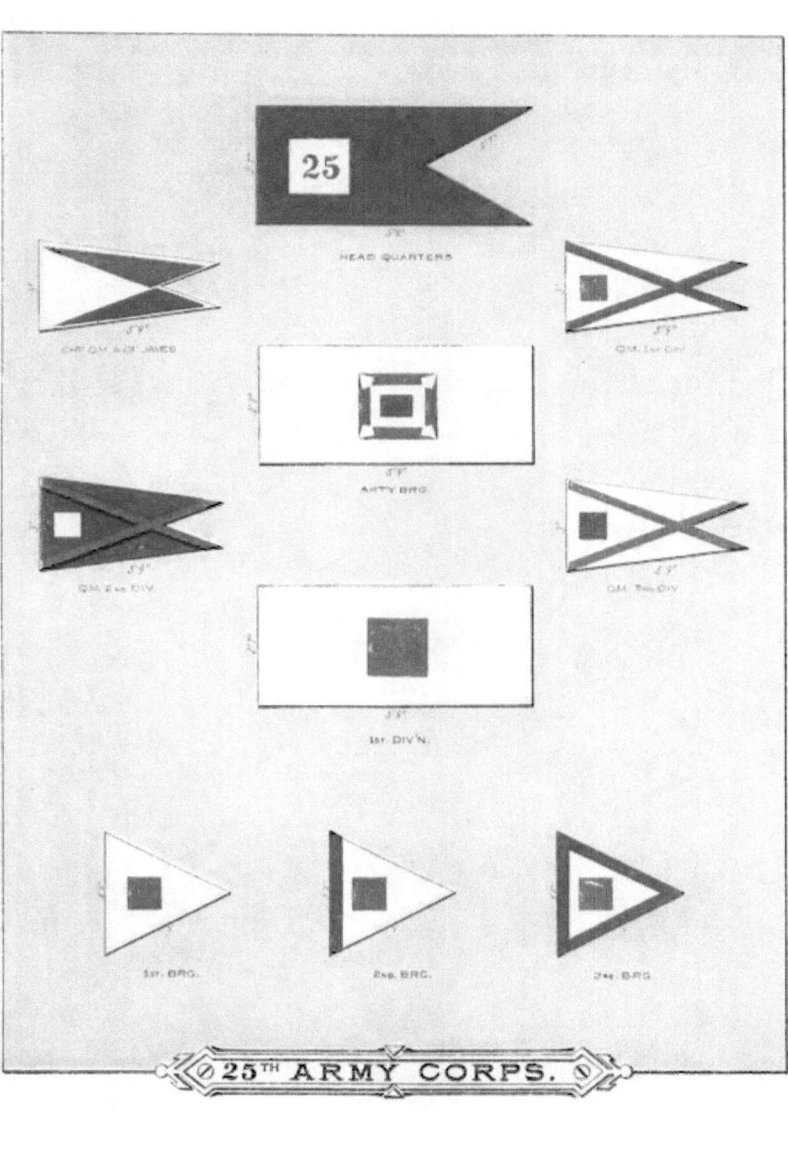

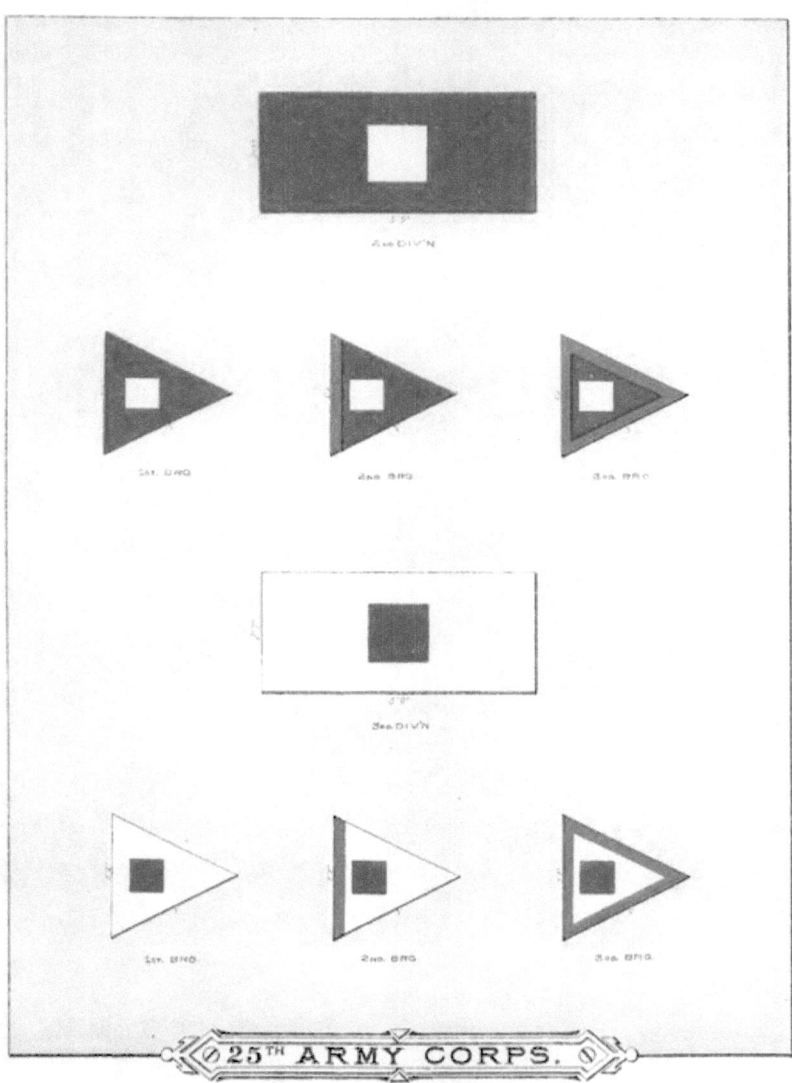

HEAD QUARTERS

ARTY BRG

SEPARATE BRG

1st BRG

2nd BRG

3rd BRG

DEP'T OF WEST VA.

ADOPTED JAN 3 RD 1865
GEN ORDER Nº 2
EXCEPT AS NOTED ON 2ND DIV

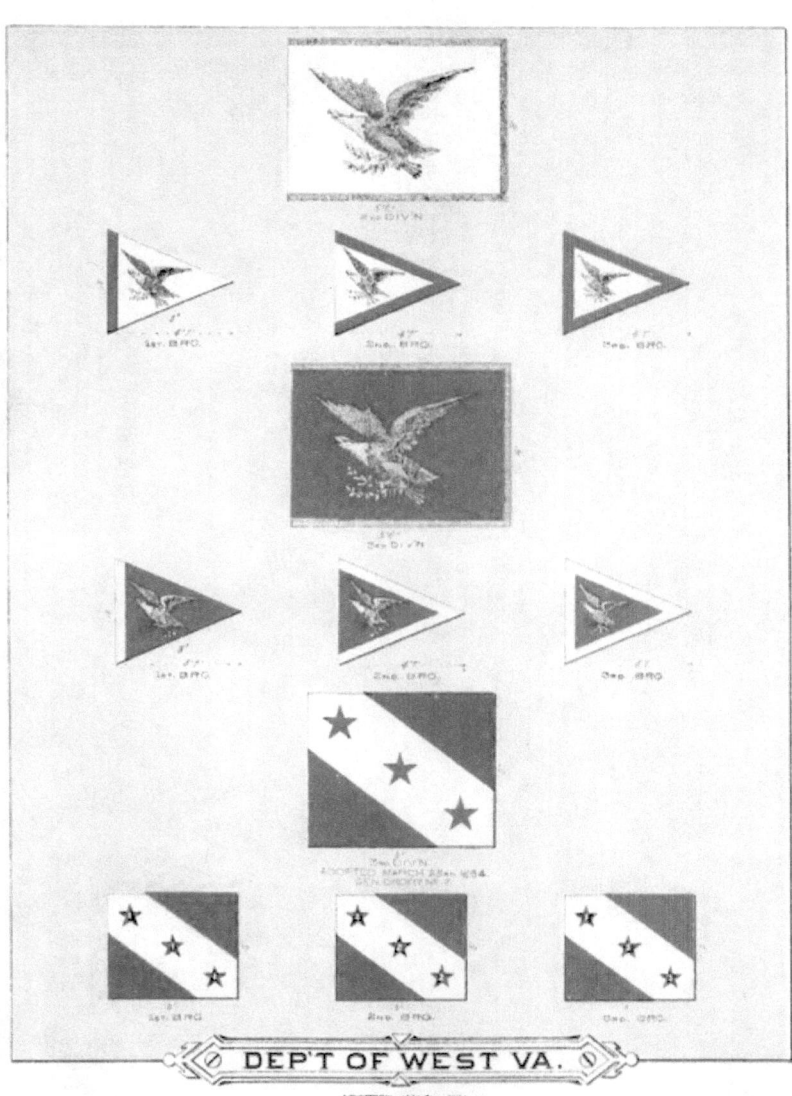

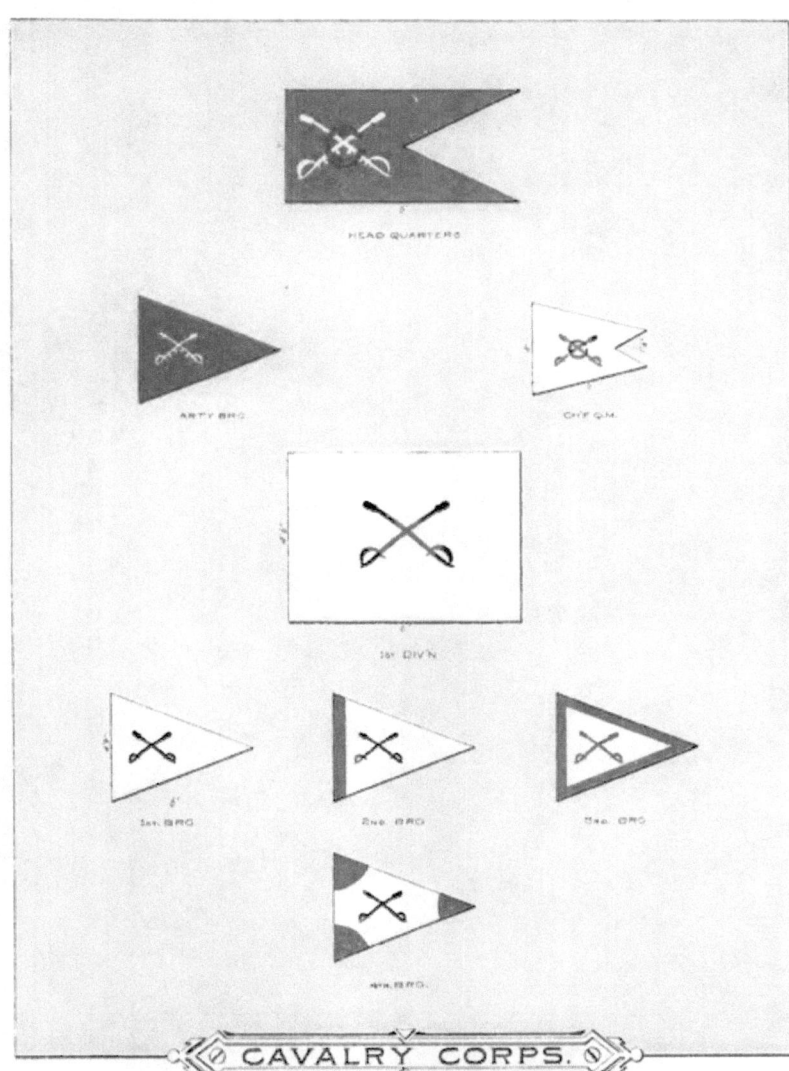

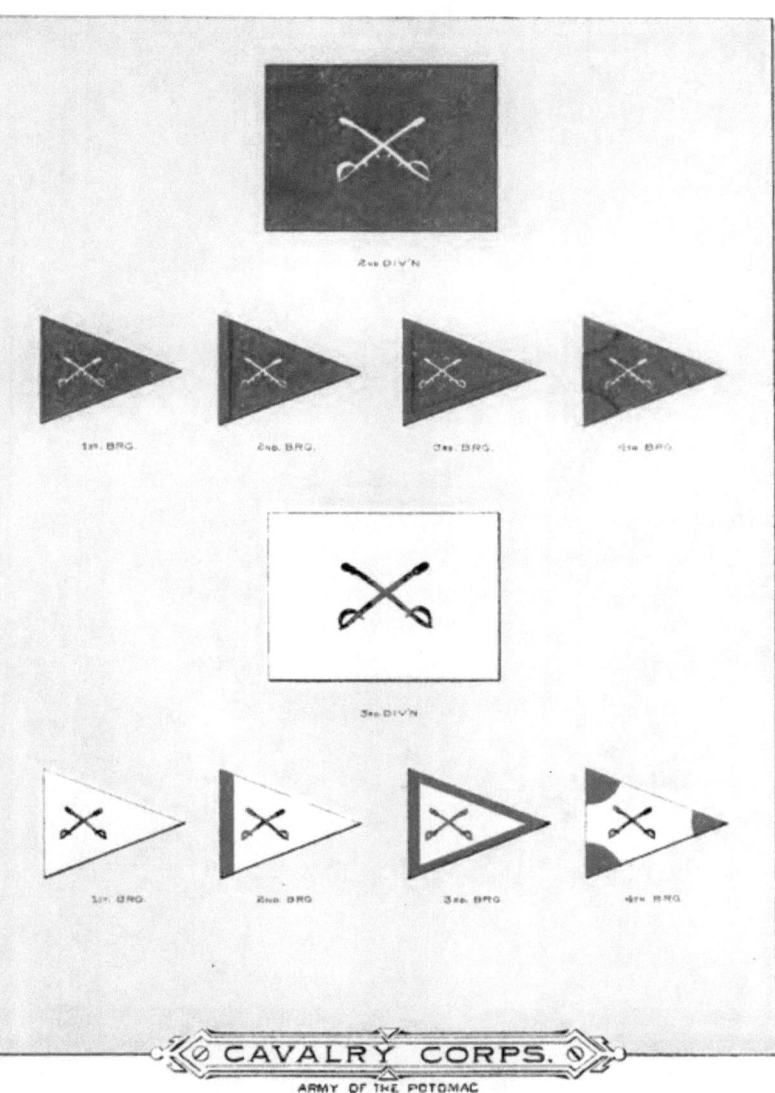

HEADQUARTERS.

1st. DIV'N.

1st. BRG.

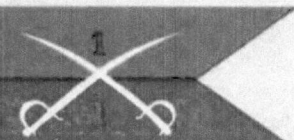
2nd. BRG.

2nd. DIV'N.

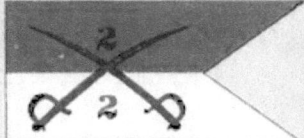
1st. BRG.

2nd. BRG.

CAVALRY CORPS.
MILITARY DIVISION OF THE MISSISSIPPI

3rd DIV'N

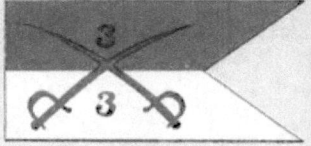
1st. BRG

2nd. BRG

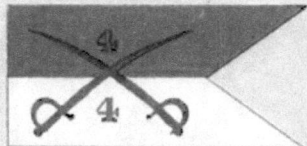
4TH DIV'N

1ST. BRG

2ND. BRG

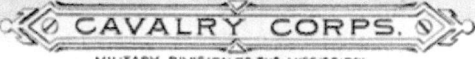

CAVALRY CORPS.
MILITARY DIVISION OF THE MISSISSIPPI

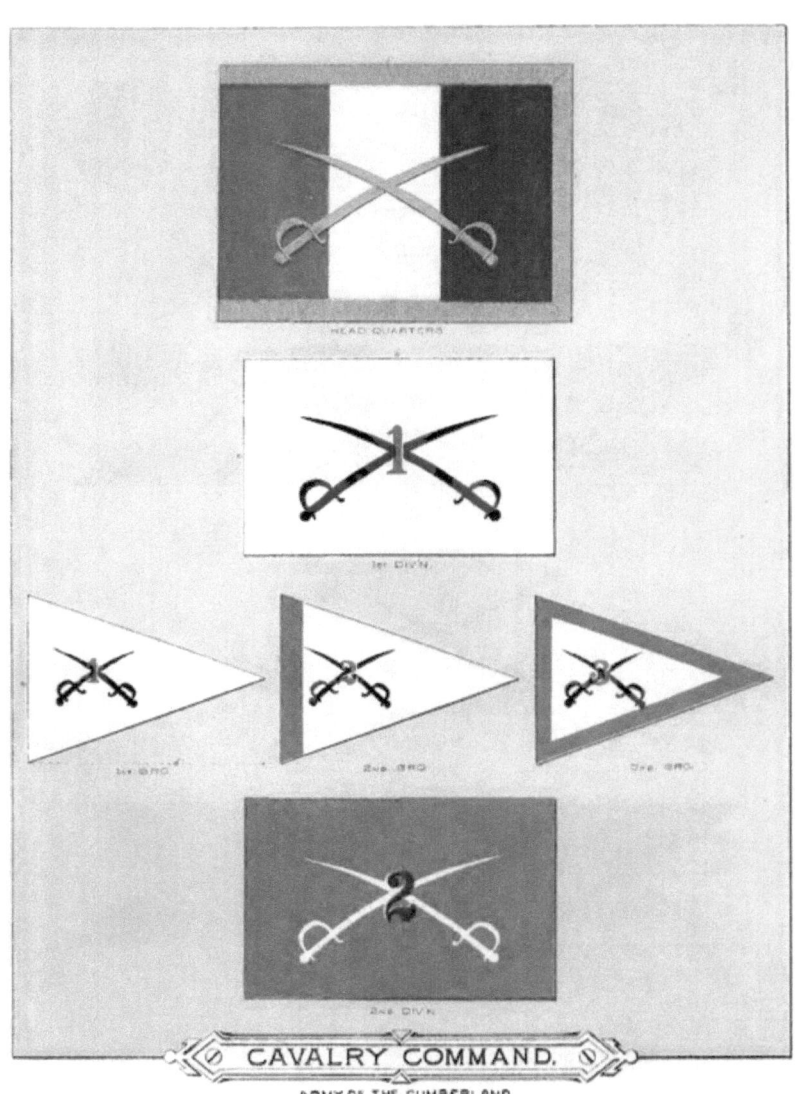

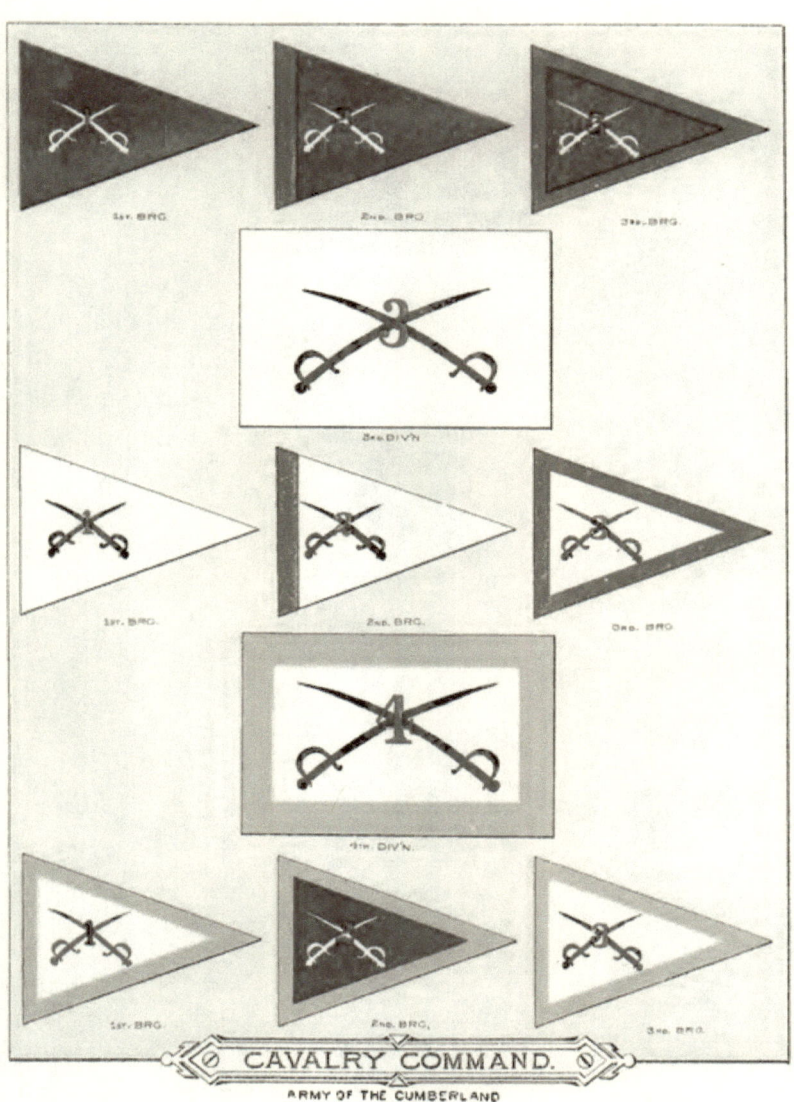

CAVALRY COMMAND.
ARMY OF THE CUMBERLAND

CORPS HEAD QRS.

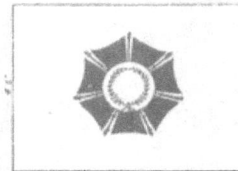
DIV HEAD QRS.

1st BRG.   2nd BRG.   3rd BRG.

1ST VETERAN ARMY CORPS.

CHIEF OF ARTILLERY.

CHIEF OF ORDNANCE.

CHIEF ENGINEER.

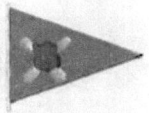
ARTILLERY BRIGADES.

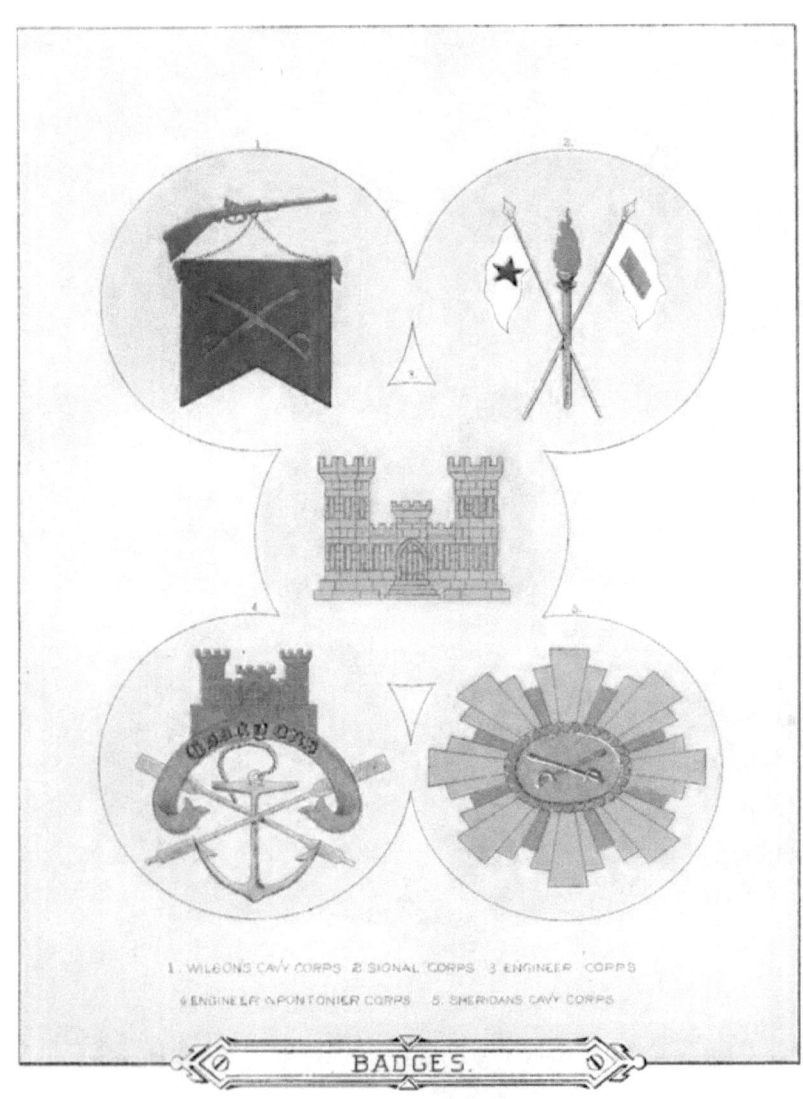

BADGES.
WORN BY MISCELLANEOUS COMMANDS

1. WILSON'S CAV'Y CORPS. 2. SIGNAL CORPS. 3. ENGINEER CORPS.
4. ENGINEER & PONTONIER CORPS. 5. SHERIDAN'S CAV'Y CORPS.

www.ingramcontent.com/pod-product-compliance
Lightning Source LLC
Chambersburg PA
CBHW020309170426
43202CB00008B/559